Simply Nietzsche

Simply Nietzsche

PETER KAIL

SIMPLY CHARLY
NEW YORK

For Cheryl: Amor Fati

Contents

Praise for *Simply Nietzsche*

"This is the best introductory text on Nietzsche in English, German or French, and in three respects: it is genuinely introductory without being superficial; it reflects good philosophical judgment; and it stakes out interesting and plausible hypotheses on some vexed questions of interpretation. The writing is also crisp and engaging throughout."

–Brian Leiter, Karl N. Llewellyn Professor of Jurisprudence, Director of the Center for Law, Philosophy, and Human Values, The University of Chicago

"Peter Kail has written a lively and intelligent short guide to Nietzsche's remarkable corpus. Best of all he does not make this singular philosophical genius conform to the dreary character of so much academic philosophy. Instead, Nietzsche the profound psychologist and writer of great distinction shines through."

–Keith Ansell-Pearson, Professor of Philosophy, University of Warwick

"This is an admirably readable, philosophically-astute introduction to Nietzsche's thought."

–Andrew Huddleston, Reader in Philosophy, Birbeck College, University of London

"Kail's *Simply Nietzsche* offers a clear and admirably concise overview of the central themes in Nietzsche's work. It is highly accessible and is written in a lively, conversational style. It would be an excellent introductory guide for students."

–Paul Katsafanas, Associate Professor of Philosophy, Boston University

"Peter Kail's introduction to Nietzsche offers a brisk, informed, and sympathetic approach to this philosophical giant. The book is something of a *tour de force*. In seven short, lucid chapters it manages to cover the full extent of Nietzsche's most significant writings from *The Birth of Tragedy* to *Ecce Homo*, leaving no philosophical stone unturned. A perfect companion for students, teachers, or novices who are just curious to know what makes Nietzsche so compulsively readable despite his being the most challenging thinker since Kant. Nietzsche will turn your life upside down. *Simply Nietzsche* will help you get your bearings as you land back in reality."

–James I. Porter, Irving G. Stone Professor in Literature and Professor of Rhetoric and Classics, UC Berkeley

"Few philosophers have left a more enduring mark in the popular imagination, and none has been more frequently caricatured or misunderstood, than Friedrich Nietzsche. To correct this misrepresentation, we needed a writer possessed of a deep knowledge of the increasingly sophisticated philosophical scholarship devoted to his thought and capable of making it at once accessible and appealing to a broad readership. In Peter Kail, we have found just such a writer. This short book gives a clear, concise, and well-informed overview of Nietzsche's main philosophical insights, which corrects common misunderstandings of them, emphasizes their originality, and acknowledges their lingering problems."

–Bernhard Reginster, author of *The Affirmation of Life* and Professor of Philosophy, Brown University

"Peter Kail gives us an exceptionally lucid, accessible and judicious introduction to a thinker whose real views often differ radically from those his reputation suggests—and are all the more interesting for that."

—Stephen Mulhall, Professor of Philosophy, New College, Oxford University

"*Simply Nietzsche* is arguably the best contemporary introduction to Nietzsche on the market and will, without doubt, be read by generations. While there are plenty of admirable, often longer introductions out there, *Simply Nietzsche* bears the hallmarks of a philosopher who first honed his philosophical acumen on the likes of Hume and Berkeley before turning, with a critical eye, to Nietzsche. In enviable lucidity, Peter Kail introduces both the novice and the experienced reader to a consistent and attractive interpretation. In exciting prose, he offers a careful selection of key works, concepts, and arguments, without ignoring their challenges, their inconsistencies, and Nietzsche's deliberately emotionally-charged style. *Simply Nietzsche* not only introduces Nietzsche's philosophy, but it also shows how one should go about reading the philosopher who has wrong-footed so many."

—Manuel Dries, Senior Lecturer in Philosophy, The Open University

Other *Great Lives*

Series Editor's Foreward

S imply Charly's "Great Lives" series offers brief but authoritative introductions to the world's most influential people—scientists, artists, writers, economists, and other historical figures whose contributions have had a meaningful and enduring impact on our society.

Each book provides an illuminating look at the works, ideas, personal lives, and the legacies these individuals left behind, also shedding light on the thought processes, specific events, and experiences that led these remarkable people to their groundbreaking discoveries or other achievements. Additionally, every volume explores various challenges they had to face and overcome to make history in their respective fields, as well as the little-known character traits, quirks, strengths, and frailties, myths and controversies that sometimes surrounded these personalities.

Our authors are prominent scholars and other top experts who have dedicated their careers to exploring each facet of their subjects' work and personal lives.

Unlike many other works that are merely descriptions of the major milestones in a person's life, the "Great Lives" series goes above and beyond the standard format and content. It brings substance, depth, and clarity to the sometimes-complex lives and works of history's most powerful and influential people.

We hope that by exploring this series, readers will not only gain new knowledge and understanding of what drove these geniuses, but also find inspiration for their own lives. Isn't this what a great book is supposed to do?

Charles Carlini, Simply Charly
New York City

Preface

Friedrich Wilhelm Nietzsche (1844-1900) is one of the most brilliant, controversial, misunderstood, vilified, recognizable, engaging, provocative, and complicated philosophers ever to have put pen to paper. The bare bones of his biography are as follows: his father, Karl Ludwig, was a Protestant clergyman; his mother's name was Franziska. He had a sister, Elisabeth (about whom I will say a little more later), and a brother, Joseph, who died very young. This tragedy was compounded by the fact that Nietzsche's father passed away when Friedrich was only six, precipitating the family's move to Naumburg. In 1864, he went to Bonn University, moving to Leipzig in 1865. Nietzsche's initial studies were in theology and philology, though he soon dropped the former subject. After a brief and harrowing period of military service, he returned to Leipzig, and, in 1869, he was elected Associate Professor of Classical Philology in Basel, Switzerland. The following year, he became a full professor, partly owing to the influence of his teacher, Friedrich Ritschl. Nietzsche was only 24, which appears an astonishing appointment for one so young. But although many see early signs of the recognition of Nietzsche's genius in such a precocious appointment, it should be remembered that the university in Basel was in great financial trouble and took the expedient of employing those whom it could pay little, which meant employing the young.

Two significant encounters predate his election to his professorship. One was his discovery of the philosophy of Arthur Schopenhauer, whose influence, though most prominent in Nietzsche's early work, never left Nietzsche's mind. The second was a personal encounter with the composer Richard Wagner, with whom he became friendly, visiting him and Wagner's wife, Cosima, for a three-year period. It was to be a very significant, intense, but relatively short-lived relationship. Nietzsche initially idolized Wagner, and, perhaps, also fell in love with Cosima. There was much intellectual discussion between the three of them, an exchange of ideas that would be crucial to Nietzsche's first book, *The Birth of Tragedy Out of the Spirit of Music*, a work that, among other things, is a near apotheosis of Wagner. But disillusionment followed as we shall see in later chapters, and for the rest of his sane life, Nietzsche wrote of Wagner as the personification of the problems of modernity. Disillusion, too, as again we shall see later, came in respect to his role as a university professor, as did ill health, which was to dog him for the rest of his life.

The publication of *The Birth of Tragedy* (1872) met with vilification and incredulity from the academic community, especially since Nietzsche had a reputation as a brilliant and promising young philologist in the rigorous German mold. It was "sheer nonsense," declared one professor, and students were advised to avoid Nietzsche's classes. And avoid his classes they did. Despite this, and his increasingly poor health, he remained in post until retiring in 1879 on a modest pension. But he continued to write, penning four lengthy essays, published separately, but which together comprise *Untimely Meditations*, and another book, *Human, All Too Human: A Book for Free Spirits* (1878).

The period beginning with the publication of *Human, All Too Human* is often referred to as Nietzsche's "middle period." Intellectually, it breaks from Schopenhauer and Wagner, and it is also close to a break in his domestic arrangements: his retirement meant more travel in search of (elusive) relief from his headaches and vomiting. He spent time in Sorrento, Italy; Nice, France; as well as in Swiss resorts of St. Moritz and Sils Maria, a place that would become his summer home, and where there is now a Nietzsche museum. Despite his medical problems, he was productive, publishing two major works in quick succession—*Daybreak* (1881) and *The Gay Science* (1882). Although he was prolific, he was not successful. His books did not sell well, something that, naturally, displeased him. A different, and rather dramatic, disappointment occurred in 1882 when he traveled to Rome with his friend Paul Rée. Rée introduced Nietzsche to a 21-year-old Russian woman, Lou

Andreas-Salomé. She was brilliant and highly independent, spurning numerous proposals of marriage in order to maintain her independence. She would later become an intimate friend of Rainer Maria Rilke and Sigmund Freud. The relationship between Salomé, Nietzsche, and Rée was initially conceived of intellectual venture—or adventure. She floated an idea for the three of them, and perhaps others, to live together for a year as an intellectual community. Nietzsche fell head over heels in love with her and instructed Rée to propose on his behalf, a proposal that Salomé declined. Unbeknownst to Nietzsche, his emissary too had fallen in love with her. The three traveled together for a while, and after they returned to their respective bases, each man was sending Salomé love letters. Nietzsche managed to persuade Salomé to visit him in Tautenburg, where the two would talk about philosophy and their common loss of Christian faith. All the time, however, she was in communication with Rée. Nietzsche's sister, Elisabeth, also contributed to his woes. Jealous of Salomé, she made the relationship even worse, reporting of Salomé's alleged slandering of Nietzsche's character to her brother and their mother and souring his relations with them as well. Nietzsche was devastated by all this and oscillated between anger and self-pity.

The period after 1882 is referred to as Nietzsche's "later" period. It begins with his most infamous work, *Thus Spoke Zarathustra: A Book for Everyone and No One*. Parts I and II were published in 1883, Part III followed in 1884, and Part IV the following year. In 1886, he published *Beyond Good and Evil, A Prelude to a Philosophy of the Future*. A year later, one of his most studied works, *On the Genealogy of Morality*, was released, expanding on key themes from *Beyond Good and Evil*. Nietzsche's last productive year was 1888 when he also spent time in Turin. It was a period of stupendous productivity: he penned *The Case of Wagner; A Musician's Problem; The Twilight of the Idols, or How One Philosophizes with a Hammer; The Anti-Christ*, the autobiographical (and much more than that) *Ecce Homo; How One Becomes What One Is*, and a compilation of his reflections on Wagner, *Nietzsche Contra Wagner*. But just at the point when Nietzsche's work was gaining recognition, he collapsed.

As well as his continuing physical ill heath, Nietzsche's behavior had become erratic: he wrote somewhat unhinged letters, which he sometimes signed as "The Crucified" or "Dionysis." He could be seen dancing and singing naked in his room. Then, as one story goes, on January 3, 1889, while in Turin, Nietzsche witnessed a man whipping a horse, and interposed himself between the horse and man, sobbing, and finally collapsing. Whatever the truth of that story, he was committed to a sanatorium in Basel on January 10, and then he was transferred to Jena, Germany, to be near his mother. His manic depression transformed itself into psychosis. Some claim that Nietzsche was suffering from syphilis, and others attribute his behavior to a non-malignant brain tumor. Whatever the cause, the remaining 11 years of his life were horrible. He moved back into the house where he had spent most of his childhood to be cared for by his mother. His physical health declined in step with his mental health, and he was wheelchair-bound by 1891, reduced to uttering random sentences rather than expressing coherent thoughts.

Ironically, as Nietzsche's health was declining, his fame was growing. An edition of his complete works was in production under the editorship of his longtime friend Heinrich Köselitz. Köselitz was important to Nietzsche. As Nietzsche's eyesight failed, his friend read to him and wrote his dictation; in turn, Nietzsche admired Köselitz's music, giving him the pseudonym "Peter Gast," probably a reference to Mozart's *Don Giovanni*. However, Nietzsche's sister interfered again, this time by aggressively taking the rights to Nietzsche's work away from his mother, sacking Köselitz, and founding a Nietzsche Archive in Naumburg. She then moved to Weimer, taking herself and, as one biographer, Julian Young, poignantly puts it, "the remnants of her brother." Elisabeth was an antisemite and began to control Nietzsche's image, mythologizing him according to her rather nasty conception of the world. She was responsible for the publication of the pseudo-work, *The Will to Power*, a book based on a project that Nietzsche abandoned and which she stitched together from notes not intended for publication. Nietzsche died on August 25, 1900, perhaps fortunate in not knowing that his ideas were being wilfully distorted by his sister. More distortion and misunderstanding were to come, quite at odds with Nietzsche's injunction in his autobiographical *Ecce Homo* that "I am the one who I am! Above all, do not mistake me for anyone else!"

Interpreting Nietzsche's works

Nietzsche himself is partly to blame for being so misconstrued. He anticipated as much, however. The question "Have I been understood?" sometimes punctuates his writing, and he claimed to be understood by "very few." His being misunderstood, ironically, owes itself in no small measure to the very engagingness of his writing, and facility for pithy, endlessly quotable turns of expression. Many, but by no means all, of his books appear to be unordered collections of short passages, a fact that can encourage the unwary reader to pluck out a Nietzsche quotation to fit their own predilections. Nietzsche's engaging, amusing, and sometimes provocative style partly explains why he figures in popular culture in a way unmatched by other philosophers. Innumerable pop songs invoke variants of Nietzsche's dictum from *The Anti-Christ* that "whatever doesn't kill you makes you stronger," as do equally innumerable films (Heath Ledger's Joker uttering "Whatever doesn't kill you simply makes you stranger" in *The Dark Knight*, a personal favorite of mine). Films by Woody Allen, Mel Brooks, and many others either quote directly or riff on some perceived Nietzschean theme, and there is a video game named *Beyond Good and Evil*. Expressions such as the Death of God, the Will to Power, the Overman, and the Eternal Recurrence of the Same carry with them an appealing veneer of profundity even for those who have not read a word of Nietzsche. His very striking physical image and his collapse into madness embody, and perhaps have created, a stereotype of a philosopher for many.

All this is harmless, relatively speaking. But, as we shall see in a little more detail throughout this book, the content of some of Nietzsche's claims can be engagingly and provocatively styled, but also exceedingly uncomfortable. At times, he seems concerned with very few superior individuals, condemning the rest of humanity as merely "physiologically sick" members of the "herd," the many "slaves" comparing unfavorably to the few "masters." In the 1920s, two University of Chicago students, Nathan Leopold and Richard Loeb, read Nietzsche as a confirmation of their intellectual superiority, which exempted them from the restraints of morality. Convinced that they were the superior human beings to whom Nietzsche sometimes refers, they embarked on a crime spree that ended in the kidnapping and murder of the 14-year-old Bobby Franks, a crime they conceived to be "perfect." This "crime of the century" was followed by the "trial of the century," where their defense lawyer put in a plea of guilty, but tried to persuade the jury that both boys were mentally ill.

The story of Leopold and Loeb is fascinating in its own right, but it demonstrates that careless readings of Nietzsche can inflame some dark minds. And not only careless reading: as I noted above, careful management and editing by Nietzsche's sister resulted in him becoming the figurehead of the right-wing movement, which his sister supported. Because of this intentional (mis)appropriation, Nietzsche became known as the official philosopher of the Nazi party, a painful irony since he decried German nationalism and anti-semitism in equal measure. Even before his death, Nietzsche was being exploited by Elisabeth for the cause of German nationalism, and she was very successful in this endeavor. Copies of *Zarathustra* were distributed to German soldiers during World War I, and later Hitler would visit and fund Elisabeth's Nietzsche Archive and attend her funeral. This is not to say that Nietzsche's writings are not susceptible to misrepresentation: he refers to "blonde beasts," and "Jewish hatred," praising aristocracy and referring to the "masters." But as we shall see, these expressions, when placed in context, are far from the ideology of National Socialism.

Unquestionably, Nietzsche's writings afford some unpalatable interpretations and allow for readings that are, either consciously or not, selective. While it is clear that a considered reading of Nietzsche shows that delusions of fascism and the fantasies of Leopold and Loeb are unsustainable, this does not mean that Nietzsche's opinions are congenial to modern liberal sensibilities. Further, that Nietzsche's views can be misunderstood because they are liable to selective readings, a problem that is not fixed simply by the sensible advice not to be selective. Nietzsche is certainly a radical philosopher. But it is worth dwelling on another selective reading of Nietzsche's texts, one that has given readers some license to print fiction. In an early, unpublished essay by Nietzsche, entitled "On truth and lies in a non-moral sense" (circa 1872), he writes that truth is a "mobile army of metaphors, metonyms ... illusions that are no longer remembered as being illusions." Coupled with remarks such as "there are no facts, only interpretations," a post-modern Nietzsche was fabricated, one that is also sometimes coupled with the claim that there are no facts about what Nietzsche really said or, indeed that there is a Nietzsche. All interpretations are equally "valid," since there is no such thing as truth, and what passes for knowledge and objectivity is just a matter of power relations. Then Nietzsche himself becomes merely another interpretation. Nietzsche is not merely a fascist but an irrationalist hero, a prophet of unreason.

This is a myth, like the myth that Nietzsche's philosophy is little different from the ideology of the Nazi party, but these are fallacies that enter popular consciousness and can make Nietzsche even more difficult to understand by planting expectations into the mind of the reader. With these expectations, the reader finds what he or she already assumes to be there. Such assumptions, then, need to be put aside, and we must remember other things when reading Nietzsche. The first is that he gives advice in various places about how to read him. It is not always clear what he means on first reading, and he tells us that one should read and reflect: one "must almost be a cow" and ruminate on the text. Second, Nietzsche's views change across time, and, though certain themes and problems recur throughout his career, it would be a grave error to run passages together from, for example, *The Birth of Tragedy* and the *Twilight of the Idols*. Third, Nietzsche's language is sometimes strident and rhetorical, carefully crafted to provoke a reaction in the reader. At first blush, this looks the very opposite of how a philosopher should write—in a cold and dispassionate manner. This aspect of Nietzsche's style is no accident, however. One needs to remember that many philosophers adopt styles that reflect their own philosophical positions. Baruch Spinoza's *Ethics* is written as a form of geometrical proof, expressing his conviction that the universe is a rationally ordered place. Ludwig Wittgenstein's *Philosophical Investigations* is arranged in a "criss-cross manner," reflecting his conviction that natural language is unmotley and organic, and his style is connected with what he conceives of as a "therapeutic" project of dissolving philosophical problems, which he takes to be unreal inventions of philosophers with a wrong of view of language. Nietzsche's sometimes rhetorical and strident tone, most evident in the *Genealogy*, reflects his philosophy in a number of different ways. First, as we shall see, he holds that human beings are guided unconsciously by deeply held and conflicting value judgments rather than by what might appear to be reason. The harshness of his language is a way of bringing such values to one's consciousness. Second, it can also cause a conflict of values within any person. Nietzsche talks about "masters" and "slaves," and the first impression is that he is all for the "masters" and that the "slaves" are despicable. Depending on the reader, one can be horrified at his glorification of warriors or thrilled by it. But on a second or third reading—after "rumination"—one can see that the "masters" and "slaves" are painted in much more ambiguous hues, and one's views of them become more mixed with the recognition of being pulled in one emotional direction and simultaneously pushed in the other. Third, Nietzsche also has "therapeutic" aims because he thinks modern morality is potentially harmful to those people he refers to as the "higher types" and he wants to free them from its hazard. One way to free them to do this is to alter their affects–their feelings, attitudes, and value judgments–and his rhetorical style is precisely aimed at achieving this.

One final point before we leave this preface: Nietzsche was a prolific writer, and we are left not only with his published works, but also with a huge amount of unpublished material known as the *Nachlass*. I mentioned above that Elisabeth fabricated an entire work from these notes, and, later, the philosopher Martin Heidegger claimed, in a perverse move driven by his own philosophical preoccupations, that all Nietzsche's real philosophy is in the *Nachlass* and not in the works Nietzsche published during his lifetime. The *Nachlass* can be an invaluable resource, but we must treat it with care. Nietzsche carefully crafted his published books, and so there is every reason to think of them–and not the mass of notes he left behind–as authoritative. So let us turn to his published works.

Peter Kail
Oxford, England

1. Beginnings: *The Birth of Tragedy* and *Untimely Meditations*

In 1886, Nietzsche published the second edition of his first book, *The Birth of Tragedy* (BT). Fourteen years had elapsed since the first edition. Nietzsche amended the full title of the work from *The Birth of Tragedy out of the Spirit of Music* to *The Birth of Tragedy, Or: Hellenism and Pessimism*, adding to it a preface entitled "An Attempt at Self-Criticism." I will say something about the significance of the change of title a little later, but the reader will recall from the Preface to this book that *The Birth of Tragedy* was, to put it mildly, ill-received ("sheer nonsense" was one sneering response, as I mentioned). But there are few sterner critics of the work than the Nietzsche of 1886. BT is, he writes, "an impossible book," one that it is "badly written, clumsy, embarrassing, with a rage for imagery. "It is "an arrogant and wildly enthusiastic book," "too arrogant to prove its assertions, mistrustful even of the *propriety* of proving things." Let us look at this "impossible book" by asking what it is about.

When Nietzsche wrote BT, he was under the sway of Schopenhauer's philosophy, as well as Wagner's music and philosophy. It is vital to know a little about each to understand Nietzsche's "impossible" book. We begin with a brief account of Schopenhauer's thought. His *magnum opus* is the two-volume *The World as Will and Representation*, which Nietzsche found in a bookshop in Leipzig in 1865. The central claim of this book is remarkable: the world as we ordinarily experience it, and think it to be, is essentially a form of *appearance* organized and constituted by our consciousness. There is a world that is not mere appearance, but what we can experience and think of are characteristic forms of appearance, objects like rivers and trees, that partly depend on us for their existence. Our conscious life, our world of daily experience, is in many ways analogous to a dream, an illusion of sorts different from how the world really is. Individual things–tables, chairs, trees, or rocks–are related in space and time by causality; however, space, time and causality, and things they relate to exist only "for us." Space, time, causality, and individuality are only how we "carve up" a world in which there is really no space, time, causality, or individuality. In this respect, Schopenhauer is following the broad outlines of the philosophy of Immanuel Kant. We cannot conceive of the world except in terms of its projecting a certain kind of appearance to us, and so the "empirical world"–the world of experience in which we live–is mind-dependent.

This, however, leaves the world "in itself." The world, that is, that stands beyond the appearances experienced by us. What could be said about that? Kant argues that we can say nothing because we cannot even form *thoughts* about it. To think of an object is to think in terms of how it *appears* to you or another mind, so one cannot think of it as it is in itself. It is just a "something"–the "thing in itself.".

Schopenhauer, however, argues otherwise. Everything in our world is a certain form of appearance, the way the world "in itself" shows up to us. This includes our own bodies. So, for example, our limbs are "appearances." But, Schopenhauer says, we stand in a special relationship to our own bodies. On the one hand, our body is just like any other physical object, located in space and time, and subject to causal laws. On the other hand, we have immediate control of our bodies through our will. This offers a dual perspective on our bodies: they are at once objects in the natural world (which, remember, are appearances) and also something that our will has direct control over. Schopenhauer thinks this dual perspective shows that the world in itself is just the *will*, a blind striving, analogous to our striving, but extending to the entire cosmos. The things we perceive and think about, are really the "objectifications" of this blind, striving force.

This will strike many a reader as a very odd claim, and we shall see how its presence is felt in BT in due course. But there is in

Schopenhauer's system a more concrete claim about how the human will is constituted, which leads him to a different philosophical position, that of *pessimism*. The world in itself is striving or will; therefore, what we are—and what all living things are—is striving. We are living things, and living things are always and essentially striving things. But there is a different question to be asked: we are living things, but is it worth living? This is a central question for Schopenhauer: does existence have a value? In other words, is it better to live than not to live?

His answer is negative: existence has no value in itself. A "life, by its whole tendency and disposition, is not capable of any true bliss or happiness, but is essentially suffering in many forms and a tragic state in every way." Living creatures oscillate between painful desire and striving and boredom. It may seem that happiness is achieved when one gains what one desires, but, according to Schopenhauer, what that achieves is merely the cessation of the painful desire. "Happiness" is merely the negative state of the removal of pain. This "happiness" does not remain long, however. We become bored, and our painful wants propel us forward again to some other goal. How can we relieve ourselves of boredom and suffering, apart from simply committing suicide? One temporary respite from the suffering that is "the essence" of life is the aesthetic experience of beauty and the arts. It lifts us away from the striving of the will, releasing us from its painful effects, and leading to something like a tranquil state. Art can help us escape from the "essence of life," "the suffering of the ever-striving will.

We are not quite done with Schopenhauer, and we will come to Wagner shortly, but first, we will turn to Nietzsche. BT is an elaborate attempt to provide an answer to pessimism. Nietzsche saw in Greek culture a clear-eyed perception of the truth of pessimism, enshrined in the wisdom of Silenus. King Midas sought from Silenus, the mythological tutor of wine God Dionysus, an answer to the question of what is the best and most excellent thing for human beings. The answer, Nietzsche reports, is that the "very best thing is utterly beyond your reach not to have been born, not to *be*, to be *nothing*. However, the second best thing for you is: to die soon" (BT 3). Yet at a certain stage of their culture, the Greeks could appreciate this truth and respond to it in the best possible way in the form of tragedy and, above all, in the tragedies of Aeschylus and Sophocles. The only viable response to pessimism is aesthetic, which resembles Schopenhauer's invocation of aesthetic responses to pessimism, but in a way very different from Schopenhauer's version.

For Nietzsche, the answer lies in the high point of Greek tragedy embodying and revealing the fundamental truth that "only as an aesthetic phenomenon is existence and the world eternally *justified*" (BT 5). How did the Greeks arrive at this answer? Here again, the influence of Schopenhauer is clear. Nietzsche claims to identify two forces at work in Greek culture, analogous to Schopenhauer's world of appearance and world as will, which, though in opposition, conspire to produce tragedy. These he named after the deities of Apollo and Dionysos. The Apollonic is Nietzsche's version of representation, the Dionysiac his version of will. In some moods, at any rate, Schopenhauer is prepared to talk of the world as representation, an illusion, or a dream, a veil placed on the world that is really the will. One reason it is thought to be a "dream" or "illusions" is that it makes us experience a world of distinct, individual things, whereas the world in itself is really a single thing. Nietzsche uses Schopenhauer's term *"principium individuationis*," the "principle of individuation" in connection with the Apollonic (BT 1). The Apollonic drive is a drive to appearance and form, exemplified in sculpture and epic poetry. The Dionysiac drive is not the blind striving of the will as it is for Schopenhauer, but is instead a drive to, or a state of, *Rausch* or "intoxication." In art that is Dionysiac, this "intoxication" or "ecstasy" is a "breakdown of the *principium individuationis*" (BT 1), we lose individuality, and glimpse the primordial unity of the world. Music is the exemplar of the Dionysiac. Nietzsche sees these drives as existing prior to any self-conscious art or artists. The drive of the Apollonic is a drive to order and restraint, the Dionysiac to excess, and breaking free of restraint. These are forces that exist in individual human beings as well, are the drives behind all art. Their opposition is itself artistically fruitful and, at its apex, produces Attic tragedy. The Apollonic, the "sculptor ... and the epic poet, are lost in the contemplation of images," while the Dionysiac musician "with no image at all, is nothing but primal pain and the primal echo of it" (BT 5).

Nietzsche discusses the Apollonic in connection with the epic poetry of Homer, and in its treatment of the gods. The important thing for Nietzsche is that Greek gods are not transcendent, otherworldly, or supreme moral exemplars in a way that Christian conceptions of God are. There is no sign of "moral loftiness" in them or "a loving gaze filled with compassion," nor anything of "spirituality and duty" (BT 3). Instead, they represent human existence, terror, and loss, the familiar human predicament but on a grander scale than the humdrum. Such gods "justify the life of men by living it themselves—the only satisfactory theodicy!" (BT 3) But art still functions at the level of dreamlike appearance, or *Schein*, and omits the Dionysiac. Tragedy is the artistic synthesis of these two aspects of human existence. The chorus of Attic tragedy, the music that is lost to us, expresses the Dionysiac and is combined with Apollonic poetry. First, tragedy involves a recognition of the terrible truth behind human existence, simply because its hero is destroyed by circumstance: there is no happy ending. Importantly, the representation of this fact is not merely in terms of the images and words of the Apollonic. The music of the chorus, and the setting of such tragedies in the context of festivals, break down the distinction between the chorus and the audience, and, indeed, the individuals comprising both. All "divisions between one human being and another, give way to an overwhelming feeling of unity which leads men back to the heart of nature" (BT 7). It affords a glimpse of the underlying, and terrible truth that lies behind the Apollonic "dream" of individuality, but a glimpse that is made, nevertheless, bearable through its Apollonic presentation. For a moment, we somehow become "the primordial being itself," and

e what is necessary "given the unaccountable excess of
of existence thrusting and pushing themselves into life, given
suberant fertility of the world-will" (BT 16). Our glimpse of
the primordial being under an aesthetic guise somehow justifies
existence to us.

Wagner, Schopenhauer, and Kant

It isn't clear quite how this is supposed to work, but maybe, as Aaron
Ridley[1] suggests, this glimpse into the fundamentally irrational
Dionysiac world somehow refreshes the spectator's own will to live.
This brings us to an aspect of Schopenhauer's philosophy I have
yet to mention, an aspect which also brings in Wagner. Music, for
Schopenhauer, is our key connection with the essence of the world,
and it is for this reason that he considers music to be in a category
of its own. Recall that the world in itself—the world beyond the
dream-like appearances of representation—is the will. The ebb and
flow of the will shows itself, albeit inchoately, in consciousness of
our own desire and action, but there is another way in which it
can be presented to us. That is through the movement of music,
in its crescendo, suspension, and iresolution. Music, Schopenhauer
tells us, is a "copy" of the will, and so the most profound of artistic
endeavors. A composer of genius does not produce a work that
expresses his or own emotions, or something equally, and merely,
as transitory; rather, he expresses the very essence of the world.
Something like this thought finds its way into BT as well, which is
why the Dionysiac is intimately bound to music. Dionysiac choral
song is the "essence of nature ... bent on expressing itself" (BT 2),
and this is why the birth of tragedy is a birth out of the "spirit of
music."

1. Nietzsche on Art, (London: Routledge, 2007)

This brings us to Wagner. As one might imagine, Schopenhauer's philosophy of music made him the darling of composers, and Wagner, like Nietzsche, was an ardent admirer of Schopenhauer. As I mentioned in the Preface, Nietzsche was a close friend of Richard and Cosima Wagner. He was present on Christmas Day 1870 when Richard gifted Cosima with his new composition, "Siegfried Idyll." Richard's philosophical views, like those of so many of his contemporaries, concerned the state of culture and society, and the need for its revitalization. He saw everywhere a pernicious fragmentation of the population into disconnected individuals, and the twin threats of consumerism and base hedonism. Something was needed to unify and elevate culture, and for Wagner, that meant a "collective artwork," or *Gesamthkunstwerk*, wherein an individual could find meaning and belonging within a united culture. He saw Greek tragedy as the model for a collective artwork. He embraced Schopenhauer's pessimism, and his view that music's disclosure of reality somehow provides an answer to pessimism. But, of course, Wagner is no mere theoretician. The inaugural Bayreuth festival of 1876, which Nietzsche helped to plan, expresses nothing short of the ambition to enact his collective artwork. The last movement of the BT—from section 16 onward—is, in effect, the claim that "rebirth of tragedy" is possible in Wagner's operas, and that the conditions of German culture make this rebirth ripe. But to appreciate why Nietzsche feels that he can make this claim, we need to look at the second movement of the BT, where he describes the forces behind the fall of the high point of Attic tragedy.

He puts the finger on two culprits, the playwright Euripides and the philosopher Socrates. Euripides, "*the thinker*, not the poet," "brought the spectator on the stage" in the sense that his heroes are more realistic and psychologically rich depictions rather than timeless heroic tropes, and that he side-lined the all-important Dionysiac chorus. Behind Euripides's drift to realism in tragedy is Socrates, whom Nietzsche sees as the personification of unbounded optimism in the power of reason. At the high point of Attic tragedy, there is an insight into and abandonment of a fundamentally irrational world. But it is against this, and indeed a conception of the world as such, that Socrates stood. He lacked entirely any mysticism and had a steadfast will to dispense with appearance. Reason was the route to wisdom and happiness. Euripides' plays reflect this optimism and so cut tragedy off from its brief disclosure of the fundamental Dionysiac character of existence. Socratism killed drama.

This death of tragedy brings with it the death of the aesthetic justification of existence. Nietzsche and Wagner see the optimism about rationality that killed tragedy as the force behind the decline in culture. One thing I have yet to mention, which is, as we shall see, a recurrent theme in Nietzsche's thought throughout his career, is the emergence of a post-Christian world. Christianity provided a way of understanding humanity's place in the cosmos that makes sense of the suffering on this earth and gives meaning to life; but rationality kills. Although Nietzsche doesn't explicitly mention Christianity in BT, it is nevertheless clear that he believes this conception of the world is no longer tenable, for at least some people at any rate, and he has an abiding concern about how we can fill the vacuum left by the end of this worldview. We shall see much more of this idea as we trace Nietzsche's intellectual career, but for the moment, we can note that this was a concern for both Nietzsche and Wagner. Part of this decline owes itself to the unbounded optimism of rationality, but there is a twist in the direction of rationality. That twist is German philosophy and particularly the philosophies of Kant and Schopenhauer. Thanks to their "enormous courage and wisdom," German philosophy offers a "victory over the optimism that lies hidden in the nature of logic and which in turn is the hidden foundation of our culture" (BT 18). The Socratic optimism, namely that reason can grasp the world in its entirety, comes up against the Kant-Schopenhauer claim I mentioned at the beginning of this chapter. The world we experience is essentially only a form of appearance; logic and causality apply only to that world. This leaves the world itself outside the realm of rational knowledge. For Kant, the limitations of knowledge mean that he could "leave room for faith," whereas Schopenhauer held that we could at least glimpse the world as the will, and glimpse it as ungoverned by reason. This allows two things. First, if the world is a representation or image, and we can never go beyond it as such, mythical image is no longer seen as illegitimate but something to be celebrated. Second, it leaves room for Nietzsche's conception of Dionysiac or the "primordial one," and the hope that Wagner's "collective artwork" will bring us back in touch with it.

More on the *Birth of Tragedy*

There is an excited and, dare I say, intoxicated air to the BT, both in its presentation and its grandiose claims. Although, as we saw, Nietzsche was one of the work's sternest critics, certain themes from BT stayed with Nietzsche for the rest of his sane life. Certainly, he became disillusioned by both Schopenhauer and Wagner, but that is not to say that he rejected wholesale every aspect of Schopenhauer's philosophy, or that he suddenly developed a strong dislike for Wagner's music. He fell out from under the spell of Wagner's personality and saw Wagner's attempt at cultural regeneration as wrongheaded. The metaphysics of Schopenhauer that makes its way, however inchoately, into the BT is something to which Nietzsche would also develop a strong antipathy. As to the book itself, the 1886 re-titling of *The Birth of Tragedy. Or: Hellenism and Pessimism* gives us a clue to what Nietzsche took to be important in the work. BT orients itself around pessimism and the Greek response to it. As Nietzsche puts it the new Preface, "An Attempt at Self-Criticism," there remains "a great question mark over the value of existence." He pondered this question mark continually throughout his career, though not in Schopenhauerian terms. The new Preface also alludes to something he terms the "pessimism of strength," and this relates to the different way that

Nietzsche would conceive pessimism later in his career. Schopenhauer, we saw, believed art constituted a temporary relief from the ceaseless striving of the will, but he also had an ethical philosophy that responded to pessimism. This ethical philosophy was one of self-denial, of ascetic renunciation of life, implying that the moral response to the suffering that is essential to life is to withdraw from life. Nietzsche became increasingly dissatisfied with this response. A pessimism of strength—as opposed to weakness in the face of suffering—is one that doesn't turn away, or withdraw, from the terrible truths of existence. One should not try to disguise or withdraw from existence, acknowledge suffering, and affirm life. It is this quality that Nietzsche saw in the Greeks. They were fully aware of the horrors of existence but continued to embrace life. They were, as he puts it in the preface to the second edition of *The Gay Science*, "superficial—Out of profundity!"

As we saw, Nietzsche charged Socratism with the death of tragedy and with contributing to the decline of culture. Socratism is also implicated in the untenability of the moral justification of the world. Reason cannot provide one, and reason also shows the moral justification given by Christianity as untenable. So, if reason cannot provide an answer, what should we do? The BT's response, as we have seen, is to reject the idea that reason can tell us all, embracing instead the Post-Kantian limitations on science as a route to understanding the world, restore the centrality of myth, and offer the spectacularly *outré* claim that collective artworks can elicit a momentary dissolution of the appearance of individual and contact with the irrational, primordial, Dionysiac One. Nietzsche quickly abandoned this response but continued thinking about the relation between science, culture, pessimism, and Christianity. After toying with skepticism about truth (which will discuss a little when we come to look at *Beyond Good and Evil*), Nietzsche became increasingly confident that science is the route to truth. He also rejected the distinction that conditioned the philosophies of Kant and Schopenhauer, namely that between the world of appearance—the empirical world—and the world as it is. But his increasing confidence in science as a route to truth should not be confused with the optimistic claim that truth will bring happiness or set us free. For him, there remains a question about the *value* of truth. Why is truth held in such high estimation? Why do we think we should have truth "at any price?" As we shall see, Nietzsche has some interesting and sometimes surprising things to say about this issue. For the time being, I will merely remark that this concern with the value of truth is linked to a threat related to, but different from, pessimism. This is the threat of *nihilism*. Pessimism places a value on existence, but a negative value: it is *better* not to exist than to exist. The terrible truth of nihilism—if it is a truth—is that existence has *no* value at all. Human beings *need* values in their lives in order to exist: but what if there is nothing of value at all?

Untimely Meditations

Nietzsche served as a medical orderly during the Franco-Prussian war of 1870–71, spending time at the front. It was a horrifying experience that changed him from someone who believed in the idea of the Prussian state to a skeptic regarding "Fatherlands." He also began to develop symptoms of the chronic illness that would dog him for the rest of his life. It is not for nothing that Nietzsche was preoccupied with the problem of suffering: he was in frequent states of discomfort, pain, and sickness, which were often crippling and agonizing. As well as physical pain, there was the pain caused by the reception of BT. It was, as we noted, harsh, although members of the Wagner cult unsurprisingly loved the work. Public pamphlets denouncing Nietzsche were circulated, and students discouraged from attending his classes. Exhausted, he excused himself from spending Christmas Day with the Wagners, a perceived slight that would mark the beginning of the end of that intense relationship. Despite his illness and disappointment, Nietzsche took on a considerable writing commitment, promising to deliver at least 13 long essays under the collective title of *Untimely Meditations* (UT) on diverse topics including education, philosophy and culture, the city, and the Christian disposition. However, the project yielded only four essays.

The first of these, "David Strauss, the Confessor and Writer" (1873), is not one of Nietzsche's proudest moments. Strauss, a German theologian, had also written a work to demystify Jesus. Entitled *The Life of Jesus* (1835/6), it left a considerable impression on the young Nietzsche, contributing to his loss of faith. Strauss's later work, however, *The Old Faith and the New* (1872), was deeply disliked by Wagner, and it is barely an exaggeration to say that a significant motivation in Nietzsche's attack on Strauss in this first *Untimely Meditation* was to please Wagner. Nietzsche tore into Strauss's style with such invective that he soon regretted the attack. When Strauss died soon after Nietzsche's essay was published, Nietzsche wrote in a letter that he hoped he "did not make his [Strauss's] last days more difficult and that he died without knowing anything of me." Beneath the invective, however, Nietzsche's concern about culture, similar to the one we noted in BT, and one which reflects his disillusionment with Prussian nationalism, underlies the first of the *Untimely Meditations*. The victory over France seemed to many a demonstration of Prussian superiority, but Nietzsche saw this as nothing but jingoism, in contrast to the genuine culture that the Bayreuth Festival promised to bring. Nietzsche still held out hopes for the rebirth of a culturally redemptive art.

The Bayreuth Festival project, however, was not going as well as was hoped, and financial backing was scarce. Wagner asked Nietzsche to write a manifesto for the project, which Nietzsche did, only to see the sponsorship committee choose a declaration by another author. At the same time, he had been working on the second *Untimely Meditations*, "Of the uses and disadvantages of history for life," which was published in 1874. Again, the topic of this essay is a concern he shared with Wagner, namely the value of historical knowledge, and relatedly, the valuable forms of history?

Nietzsche distinguishes among three kinds of history–"monumental," "antiquarian," and "critical." The "fundamental idea of the faith in humanity" (UT, p. 68) finds its expression in monumental history, which represents exemplars of human greatness. Its value to us is that one can learn "from it that the greatness that once existed was in any event once *possible*, and may thus be possible again" (UT, p.69). But simple and uncritical veneration has its dangers, and so requires tempering. The antiquarian historians focus not on the great but wish to represent everything of the past. In doing so, they can correct a tendency to turn historical representations into outright false idols by those intent on stifling the great of the modern age (Wagner, perhaps?). Unchecked, monumental history is a "masquerade costume in which their hatred of the great and powerful of their own age is disguised as satiated admiration for the great and the powerful of past ages" (UT, p.69). But antiquarian history is nevertheless "mummification" of the past, focused on the preservation rather than change. What is required is *critical* history, one concerned with neither mere preservation nor myth-making, but with a judgmental approach to the past. Properly conducted, history is "art," because it should adopt an expressively selective and evaluative stance to the past in order to contribute to the health of our present culture.

The second *Untimely Meditation* also contains the beginnings of Nietzsche's critical reflections on the notion of objectivity, about which I will make a few remarks, but discuss in a little more depth later in this book. To be objective, one might think, would be to put aside one's own values, interests, and prejudices, simply recording "what really happened," aiming to "mirror" the past. Aside from pointing out that historians deceive themselves in thinking that they do this, the very idea of approaching the past without values and interests is incoherent. To ask questions about what happened in the past, one should have some sense of what is *significant* to ask of it, and that itself is going to depend on one's values or interests. Determining an answer to, and even formulating the question as to "what really happened," will depend on whether one is interested in a political narrative, the position of women in some given age, the development of some sports team, or another aspect of history. The idea of determining "what really happened" independently of values and concerns doesn't make sense. This is *not* to say that the world does not constrain the answers to the questions in terms of facts. But without interests and values, no questions about the past could ever be formulated correctly.

The two remaining *Untimely Meditations*, "Schopenhauer as Educator" and "Richard Wagner in Bayreuth," mark the end of Nietzsche's "early period." His notebooks during that time are revealing in this regard. First, philosophically speaking, there are signs of the ideas Nietzsche would later develop and the style in which he would present them. Second, from 1874 on, critical thoughts about Wagner first emerged. "Schopenhauer as Educator," it is often correctly observed, is surprising because Schopenhauer's central philosophy, as expressed in *World and Will and Representation*, is all but absent from the essay. Nietzsche, as I mentioned, abandoned Schopenhauer's metaphysics, never to return to it. So what is the essay about? As the title suggests, it is about Schopenhauer as an educator, but not in the sense of his being a professor, nor, indeed, his particular doctrines, but as an example of someone able to set himself apart from prevailing cultural tides. The monumental history of the second *Untimely Meditations* also focuses on exemplars, and Schopenhauer educates by being an exemplar. Nietzsche admires Schopenhauer's distaste for university professors—not unsurprisingly, given Nietzsche's own disillusionment with his life in academia, as well as the fact that Schopenhauer's thought is dead set against the dominant philosophy of Hegel. But the exemplar that is Schopenhauer (which is, to a large extent, only Nietzsche's vision of him) makes a broader point, namely that culture requires great individuals—philosophers, artists, and saints—to enrich it.

There are many aspects of this general idea that I shall briefly note now, reserving a more detailed discussion for later in this book.

First, there is the now-familiar refrain that modern culture suffers from "spiritlessness" and that "all moral energy ... is at a low ebb" (UT, p.132), the causes of which Nietzsche admits are complicated, but, nevertheless, he singles out one–the oscillation between the ideals of Christianity and classical culture. Although Christian ideals have become unsustainable, their influence runs deep, precluding a simple return to the morality of the Greeks. Second, he thinks such cultural conditions are not conducive to the production of the great individuals capable of revitalizing life. It is here that the illiberal side of Nietzsche is pronounced. "Mankind must work continually at production of individual great men–that and nothing else is its task" (UT, p.161) he writes, and immediately responds to what he rightly anticipates as incredulity by posing a question to the individual reader:

"how can your life, the individual life, receive the highest value, the deepest significance?" People are willing to sacrifice themselves to the state, he notes–the memory of the Franco-Prussian war still with him–but a healthy culture is of more importance than any state, and only great individuals can revitalize culture. We ought to aim to discover, and bring into being, the conditions conducive to the growth of great individuals, he posits. Third, there are the beginnings of Nietzsche's reflections on the self. Later in his career, he puts the matter in terms of "becoming what one is." This sounds paradoxical. How can one become what one already is? Roughly, what one *is* is not some fixed self or soul, but a collection of different inclinations, desires, emotions and values, many of which pull us in different directions. To *become* what one is implies that all those conflicting elements must come together to form a unity. The "educators"–the great types whose duty it is to provide the conditions of their flourishing–provide ideals which contribute to the organization of our disparate psychic elements into something more coherent. As exemplars, they provide the best "means of finding one's self, of coming to oneself out of the bewilderment in which one usually wanders" (UT, p.130)

"Richard Wagner in Bayreuth" is an attempt, and perhaps not a successful one, at a balanced criticism of the composer and the supporters he encountered in Bayreuth. I have already mentioned that cracks were beginning to show in that relationship. Nietzsche attended rehearsals at Bayreuth and disliked the people whom he met intensely, exiting hastily and taking refuge in the countryside. He and Wagner clashed over the merits of Johannes Brahms. In "Richard Wagner in Bayreuth," Nietzsche sees in Wagner a "tyrannical" aspect that threatens to overwhelm others. But quoting Wagner frequently, as Nietzsche does, expresses an ideal of Wagner's art. Nietzsche was to claim later that the reason for his break with the composer was Wagner's introduction of Christianity into *Parsifal*, but that is unlikely. Far more probable is that Nietzsche's growing maturity allowed him to step out of the shadow of Wagner's formidable personality. Indeed, Nietzsche was to become his own man, but we would never be as happy again.

2. Turning New Ground: *Human, All too Human* and *Daybreak*

In 1886, Nietzsche wrote new prefaces to his previous works, including the one we have already quoted for BT. Two years later, he wrote his peculiar quasi-autobiography, *Ecce Homo* (EH), which was not published until 1908. In that work, he also revisited his previous writings in a section entitled "Why I Write Such Great Books." We will return to look at EH later in this book, but what Nietzsche said there about *Human, All Too Human: A Book for Free Spirits* (HAH) provides a useful entry point in this work. *Human, All Too Human*, he wrote, is the work "I used to liberate myself from things that *did not belong* to my nature." His tone "is completely changed," and there was "true progress" towards Nietzsche himself. Mistakes are "frozen to death," and the work "put[s] an abrupt end to all 'higher lies', 'idealism' [and] 'beautiful feelings.'" It was also the "moment my instinct made the inexorable decision to stop giving in, going along, and confusing me with other people." It is easy to read this as a record of his break from Wagner and Schopenhauer, as he explicitly stated in his EH summary of HAH. Nietzsche sent a copy to Wagner just as he received the libretto of *Parsifal* from the composer, and these two books crossing paths was "like the sound of swords crossing," he noted in EH. While the split between the two men didn't happen overnight, the rift occurred. Nietzsche began writing HAH within days of his hasty exit from Bayreuth and was still working on it when he saw Wagner for the last time, as the two briefly overlapped in the beautiful Italian town of Sorrento.

The first edition of HAH is dedicated to the French writer Voltaire, a significant signal that Nietzsche distanced his philosophy from Wagner's romanticism and the views expressed in BT. Voltaire was a figurehead of the optimism of the Enlightenment, of confidence in science and its role in progress. On the face of it, Voltaire embodies the Socratism Nietzsche was so skeptical of in BT, and which the Romanticism of Wagner also rejected. Voltaire was also significant with respect to the "tone" of HAH, and, indeed, one could say its tone is "French." By that I mean its style is predominantly aphoristic, its tone lighter, and, in a sense I shall presently explain, concerns itself with psychological observations, and as such, it has clear antecedents in writers known as the "French Moralists," who include Michel de Montaigne and François de La Rochefoucauld.

One sense in which HAH is an abrupt end to "idealism" is, precisely, Nietzsche's indifference to the fundamental distinction between the world of appearance and the world "in-itself," which conditions the philosophies of Kant and Schopenhauer. That is, HAH marks the end of his infatuation with transcendental idealism. As he put it the EH discussion of HAH, the "'thing-in-itself' is frozen to death." There is no more concern with some mystical contact with the "primordial one" behind the world of appearance. HAH, it seems, embodies a conception of philosophy that is very un-Kantian, one which dispenses with metaphysics and the distinction between the real world of the thing-in-itself and the merely empirical world. This is not only a matter of Nietzsche recoiling from Kant and Schopenhauer. Nietzsche did not have any formal training in philosophy—he was a philology professor, after all—but very early on his interests were turning away from philology and towards philosophy. Indeed, he applied for a philosophy professorship in 1870, and unsurprisingly, given his lack of a background in this field, was unsuccessful. Nevertheless, he continued reading extensively in philosophy and the natural sciences, and the current of thought took him away from the metaphysics of Kant and Schopenhauer and towards a broadly "naturalistic" approach to philosophy. Generally speaking, naturalism in philosophy claims that only the sciences provide genuine knowledge, and so philosophical issues should be in the spirit of the sciences. Furthermore, it embodies an attitude to ourselves: human beings are no different in kind from the rest of the natural world—we are animals, grand and sophisticated, but animals nevertheless. Nietzsche's naturalistic turn was heavily influenced by Friedrich Lange's 1865 *History of Materialism*, which put forward the view that human nature is fundamentally physiological in character, and physiological processes are just forms of physical process.

I shall describe in a little more detail what that meant for Nietzsche in a moment, but there is a further factor in his new turn, namely his friendship with Paul Rée. I mentioned Rée briefly at the beginning of this book as the man who introduced Nietzsche to Lou Andreas-Salomé, but that was not the only significant contribution he made to Nietzsche. As well as being friends for about seven years, Rée was hugely influential, intellectually speaking, on Nietzsche's change of direction. Rée had a doctorate in philosophy proper, and, like Nietzsche, initially admired Schopenhauer but rejected metaphysical approaches to the philosophy that Schopenhauer seemed to represent. Rée's writing was influential too: he wrote in a style akin to the French Moralists, as Nietzsche would do. He also adopted a psychological approach to morality and was broadly naturalistic in his approach to philosophy in general. Very early into their friendship, Nietzsche read Rée's *Psychological Observations*, so different both in style and content from the ponderous tomes of German metaphysics.

Rée, then, was philosophically and stylistically very important to Nietzsche, as well as instrumental to his fateful relationship with Lou Salomé. And they would work closely together and in a quite literal sense. He and Rée shared lodgings in Sorrento while Nietzsche continued to write HAH and Rée wrote his own *On the Origin of Moral Sensation*. There was, therefore, considerable cross-fertilization during this period and aspects of Rée's influence would never leave Nietzsche's thought, though Nietzsche's attitude to some of Rée's central claims would change in time.

Let us now turn to HAH itself. It comprises two volumes, the first of which was published in 1878 and the second in 1879. The latter is divided into two parts: "Assorted Opinions and Maxims" and "The Wander and his Shadow." Volume One is divided into groups of aphorisms, and longer passages, under general headings. The first section, "Of first and last things," announces Nietzsche's new naturalistic and anti-metaphysical ideas. Human beings are natural beings–all too human–and, importantly, the product of historical process. The mistake of previous philosophies was to see humans as having a timeless God-made nature, while, thanks to the burgeoning success of Darwin, human nature must be seen as the product of evolution. Nietzsche's approach, then, is to offer explanations of how human beliefs, practices like religion, and moral attitudes, emerged in the human animal. Most importantly, the existence of what we value most–morality, art, etc.–does not mean that there must be some higher realm of value, but instead that it must be conceived as the result of the way in which animal feelings and inclinations become changed and interpreted. Great things can have lowly origins. This idea continued to be important to Nietzsche. One of the "prejudices of philosophers," as he posited in *Beyond Good and Evil*, is the assumption that something of great value can only come from some "good" source. So, morality must have come from God, or from some perfect goodness that lies beyond the ordinary world, as Plato believed. Nietzsche, by contrast, thought that our morality comes from ordinary feelings and desires.

We will come back to morality, but the shift from the metaphysical to the human in HAH shows an interesting approach to religious matters taken up in Part 3, entitled "The religious life." Rather than trying directly to show that religious beliefs are false, Nietzsche suggests demonstrating how people might have the religious beliefs and experiences they do without presupposing the truth of those beliefs. If the truth of religion is not required to explain why people have the beliefs and the experiences they do, then we can dispense with God. Beliefs and feelings need not indicate contact with a "higher reality." Instead, ordinary feelings are misinterpreted as glimpses of the divine, a beguiling misconception that gives the mundane great significance.

The essence of modern morality

In the context of a discussion of the religious spirit, Nietzsche began his critical discourse on what he took to be the core of modern morality, namely "asceticism"–an ideal of self-denial or "selflessness." The morally ideal person disdains worldly goods and pleasures like material riches and sexual gratification; he or she is, above all else, concerned with other people. Nietzsche suggested, among other things, that behind this behavior is a more basic motive–that of control or power over one's self. In reality, then, "selflessness" is a strategy to exercise power. We all yearn for material goods, the gratification of desire, and to put ourselves before others, yet we cannot always successfully vent these urges. In place of getting what we want, we want to *control* those urges, or, even more so, deny that we *should* have or even *do* have these desires. According to Nietzsche, we are "designating the ineluctably natural as bad." Religion designates part of our nature as thoroughly bad. This was the beginning of a thought that would come to fruition in *On the Genealogy of Morality*, where Nietzsche claimed to have uncovered the psychology behind modern Western morality, and we shall look more closely at this idea when we come to that work.

It is, however, in Part 2, "On the natural history of moral sensation," where the central focus is morality, and this part shows Rée's influence to its greatest extent. Like Nietzsche's approach to religion, which seeks to explain by an appeal to psychology various religious beliefs and practices, he attempted to elucidate moral beliefs and practices psychologically, also exposing *false* interpretations of moral feelings. One putative error that Nietzsche claimed to have uncovered in HAH is the idea that we act solely for the interests of another person without any regard to our own needs. A truly *moral* action, therefore, is one that is "unegoistic." Nietzsche was very skeptical that such selfless actions exist, partly because of his diagnosis of asceticism that we touched above. But he also argued that even when one apparently acts in an altruistic way—that is, out of sole concern for another—we nevertheless act out of our *own* desires, our *own* inclinations, and our *own* values. "No one," he wrote, "has ever done anything that was solely for the sake of another and without a personal motive." This, however, is not Nietzsche at his best. It is perfectly true that we act out of our own desires, but that doesn't mean that those desires are desires *for us*. For instance, if a parent desires his son to succeed in life, he is not desiring something *for himself* but rather for his child.

A more significant error in morality for Nietzsche is the connection between moral feelings and the notion of free will. When we blame or praise a person, we feel we are justified in doing so because we think the person could have done something other than they did. We find someone *accountable* for an action only when that action is freely done. Fred *could have* kept the money for himself, instead of giving it to the beggar, or Mabel *could have* not stolen. We should only praise or blame an action when it is done from free will, and we only have free will when we could have done otherwise than what we actually did. But if we are really just complex natural, or biological creatures, then what we do is simply an outcome of natural process; we are no more able to do otherwise than what we actually do than a tree is free not to shed its leaves. The feeling of accountability, Nietzsche thought, is a mistaken interpretation of our nature, writing in *HAH* 1:39 that "[n]o one is accountable for his deeds. This is set against Kant's moral philosophy which saw the human being as somehow beyond the realm of natural causality and able to act freely. This denial of accountability, Nietzsche noted,

> is the bitterest draught the man of knowledge has to swallow.... [a]ll his evaluations, all his feelings of respect and antipathy have thereby become disvalued and false (*HAH*, 1, 107)

But Nietzsche didn't simply leave us with the taste of the bitterest draught in our mouths. He offers us a new way of thinking, or at least the beginnings of one. We have inherited erroneous attitudes towards the others and ourselves; the latter including guilt and failure to do what we should have done. We have also, as I mentioned above in relation to asceticism, condemned some of our natural instincts (we are "designating the ineluctably natural as bad"). Nietzsche hoped that in exposing the falsity of these views, his philosophy could contribute to "a new habit" of "surveying" ourselves, so it might bring forth the "wise, innocent ... man." Right now, we are the "unwise, unjust, guilt-conscious" human beings (HAH, 1, 107), but the solution to our predicament doesn't lie in becoming wise, just, or guilt-free. Our present morality is riddled with mistakes and false assumptions. Nietzsche hoped that once abandoned, a new morality would take its place.

Free spirits and other concepts

But what "new morality"? And for whom? Let us begin with the second question. The subtitle of HAH is "A Book for Free Spirits." Who are these? Part 5 of HAH, "Tokens of Higher and Lower Culture" gives us some indication of their identity. First, they are exceptional and rare. Second, the "freedom" of the free spirit is not, of course, the free will that Nietzsche squarely rejected. Instead, what makes a free spirit free is freedom *from* the constraints of morality. The free spirit "has liberated himself from tradition" (HAH 1 225). This, of course, is a descendant of the great individuals of the *Untimely Meditations*. One aspect of this freedom is freedom from the interpretation of morality as the demand for selflessness. The free spirit should "manipulate falsehood, force, the most ruthless self-interest as his instruments so skilfully he could only be called an evil, demonic being; but his objectives, which shine through here and there, would be great and good" (HAH 1 241). The free spirit knows enough of his nature and the grounds of present culture to "overcome" his own nature and that culture.

One might wonder what the positive content of the values of

the "free spirit" are. They are free *from* the culture of morality and aim at the "great and the good," but it is far from clear just what the "great and the good" is supposed to consist of. This will remain somewhat of a puzzle in understanding Nietzsche, though we shall make some progress in later chapters. But there is also a different evaluative dimension that makes its presence felt, namely a contrast between the "healthy" and "sick." A section entitled "Of the future of the physician," suggests that in the promotion of the free spirit, there is a need for someone who can offer "benevolent amputation of all the so-called torments of the soul and pangs of conscience" (HAH 1 243). This presumes that "sickness" in this context is a matter of psychological disturbance: humans are sick when they torment themselves psychologically, and our present morality somehow contributes to this torment. The free spirit becomes "healthy" when such torments are removed. This theme is picked up and amplified in the 1886 Preface to the second volume of HAH. As Nietzsche noted in that preface, the contents of the whole work comprise "*precepts of health* that may be recommended to the more spiritual natures of the generation just coming up."

HAH also makes use of what will become a very significant category for Nietzsche's conception of human nature, namely the notion of a "drive." It is certainly true that he used the term in his earlier works, but in HAH the notion takes shape. In the previous chapter, I mentioned that for Nietzsche there was no single thing that is a self which is the owner of one's thoughts, desires or feelings, but for him, a "self" is a somewhat inchoate collection of thoughts, desires, or feelings. Somewhat more precisely, the self for Nietzsche is a collection of drives. But what is a drive? Nietzsche appears to have gotten the notion from his reading of the psychology and biology of his day. To explain the various actions of plants and animals, such sciences posited causal powers, which are tendencies to produce certain affects. Nietzsche believed that humans are composed of such tendencies, grounded in our physiology. In other words, we are a collection of different causal tendencies.

That might seem relatively straightforward (though not unproblematic), but there is something initially puzzling in the way that Nietzsche talks about drives. His words may be taken to suggest that drives, these causal tendencies, themselves "know" things, "aim" at things, "interpret," and "value" things. Thus, in HAH, he wrote that "a drive without some kind of knowing evaluation of the worth of its object does not exist in man." (HAH I 32) It is as if for Nietzsche, these drives were miniature persons, things that know, interpret and value things. But in so doing, Nietzsche committed what is known as the "homunculus fallacy". Rather than explaining how the human mind thinks, perceives, desires, and everything else it does by appealing to drives, he simply claimed that drives themselves think, perceive and desire, etc. Nothing is explained, because, of course, this simply raises the question of how drives themselves think, perceive, desire, etc. However, it is premature to think that Nietzsche made such an elementary mistake. These concepts were common in the sciences of the day, disciplines which, as I mentioned earlier, he studied intensively. Nevertheless, that does not imply the homunculus fallacy, and so there is reason to think Nietzsche didn't advocate it either. Such talk is shorthand to describe complex causal processes underpinning the dynamics of the natural. We might say, for example, that trees want to reach the light, which is why they grow tall, but this expression is shorthand for the general tendency of trees favored by natural selection. We can say a drive strives for, or wants, food, but that again is shorthand for a complex causal structure that causes an animal to eat.

"Unknown to ourselves"

When Nietzsche began writing HAH, his provisional title for it was "The Ploughshare." This component of a plough (known as plow in the United States) turns compacted soil into new ground upon which fresh crops can grow. The old, trodden-in ground of his

Romanticism-inspired BT is broken with the naturalism of HAH, and the ideas within HAH represent both the soil and the seeds from which Nietzsche's thought would grow and flourish. It is fair to say that we only spot germination in HAH: there are lots of new, young, but very undeveloped thinking about that work. But the pace of growth is rapid, if his next work, *Daybreak: Thoughts on the Prejudices of Morality*, published in 1881 (D), is anything to go by. This book is sometimes published together with HAH, as if there were no significant differences between the two works, and as if Nietzsche's real shift in thinking is between D and his next work, *The Gay Science*. Certainly, there are new things in *The Gay Science*, but there are equally significant differences between HAH and D, and lots of continuities between D and Nietzsche's later works.

The first difference between HAH and D is that the dubious, and somewhat crude, claim that we only ever act out of self-interest, and so the assertion that actions are never taken out of the concern for the wellbeing of another person, is dropped. In D Nietzsche referred to two ways of "denying morality." In HAH, he had suggested that no one is moral because no one ever acts altruistically. That is one way of "denying morality." The other way—which was now Nietzsche's way—is "to deny that moral judgments are based on truths. Here it is admitted that there really are [altruistic] motives of action, but that in the way it is *errors* which, as the basis of all moral judgments, impel men to their moral actions." People act out of a sense of morality, for the sake of the wellbeing of others, but the moral values and the beliefs they have about them are riddled with errors. What are these errors?

The first stems from another view of Nietzsche's that begins in *Daybreak*. Central to his attempt to understand morality is an appeal to "custom" or "tradition" (*Sitte*). He introduced this notion at D, writing that "morality is nothing other (and therefore *nothing more!*) than obedience to customs, of whatever kind they may be." Central to "tradition" is the idea of a "higher authority which one obeys, not because it commands what is *useful* to us, but because it *commands.*" Such commands are conceived to come from a "higher intellect which here commands ... an incomprehensible, indefinite power, of something more than personal." Nietzsche envisaged with a great deal of plausibility that a tradition is maintained by obedience to a higher authority: one obeys commands of that supposed higher authority–not because one wants to do so, but simply because of the fear of the authority. One complies "despite of the private desires and advantages" that acting otherwise might serve.

This is obviously a religiously based view. There is some higher authority, some god or gods, from whom commands come, who set laws, and whom one obeys independently of one's own private desires and interests. Nevertheless, this account can explain a feature of morality that holds quite independently of any religious context. What is that feature? We believe that some moral actions are simply *required*, whatever else we might think or want. One *should*, one *ought*, save the person from drowning in the lake, quite independently of whether one merely wants to, or even if one doesn't want to. Even if the drowning person in the lake is one's bitterest enemy, morality *demands* or *requires* that one do the right thing–save the person–regardless of whether you like or hate the person. Nobody will forgive if one declares "I won't save him because I don't like him." Morality often demands what we don't want to do, and, sometimes, demands sacrifices. You *should* give money to the desperately needy person on the street, even though you were planning to spend it on a gin and tonic. Kant referred to such moral demands as "categorical imperatives"–"imperative because they are actions one *must* take (or must refrain from taking) and "categorical" because one is obliged to perform them regardless of whether one wants to do so. Such imperatives contrast with "hypothetic imperatives," things one must do *if* one has some particular want or desire. So, *if* I want to go to the movies at 6 pm, then I *must* leave my house an hour before, but that imperative–that demand on what I do–does not apply to me if I no longer want to see the film.

For Kant, moral demands were distinctive in being categorical imperatives. As such, moral demands do not depend on whether someone has any particular desires or wants and from this Kant concluded that moral demands are demands of reason alone. People vary in their wants and likes, and yet moral demands apply to everyone. What we *do* have in common is reason, and so moral demands must apply to us in virtue of our being rational creatures, regardless of our wants or likes; moral imperatives hold in virtue of our being rational. But now consider Nietzsche's hypothesis of the morality of custom. He recognized that moral requirements are like demands placed on us, applying independently of what we might want or not want to do. But rather than concluding that they are demands of reason, he explained why moral demands seem that way to us by elucidating how they emerged from tradition and authority. Even though explicit appeals to God or gods may have fallen by the wayside, moral requirements still *feel* like categorical demands. Once we understand that fact, and we no longer believe in supernatural authority, we can see that the commanding character of moral demands is based on an error.

However, this is not the only error. I mentioned that in *Human, All Too Human*, Nietzsche questioned the idea that human beings have free will. The issue of whether we have free will or not is a subject within a broader topic that philosophers call "agency." Humans are, so it seems, *agents* or *doers*. When I act, I am conscious of what I am doing: I act on *purpose* or *intentionally*. Furthermore, it is a matter of *me* doing something, as opposed to something that merely happens. When I am pushed by someone, I fall, and that is something that happens to me. But when I sit down, that is something that I do. Moreover, I act freely, at least when I am not being forced by others to do something. I choose to have a cup of tea, but I could have opted to have coffee instead. And, as we noted above, the notion of freedom of choice is intimately linked with moral responsibility. We blame a person for stealing the money only on the assumption we think she could have chosen not to do so. All of this can encourage the following conception of selves: a self is a single, simple thing, which is in control of our actions and chooses freely what to do. Furthermore, in so choosing, the self is fully aware of what he or she is doing. What is bringing about he or she is the self and its transparently conscious thoughts or intentions.

Kant thought selves are just like this and, because of their capacity for spontaneous freedom and pure rational deliberation, selves exist outside of the natural world of cause and effect. Nietzsche, by contrast, posited that we are wrong about what we are and how we act. We might *think* selves fit the description I gave in the previous paragraph, but we are mistaken. First, as we noted in the previous chapter, Nietzsche rejected the idea of the self as a single unitary thing but instead saw it as a collection of drives. One reason to consider the self as a unitary thing is because we think in terms of our *controlling* what we do and think. There must be a single thing that stands above our beliefs, desires, and actions and, sometimes, at any rate, assesses, assents or prevents our action. Furthermore, there is a tendency to think this single self is constituted by our *intellect* or *reason*. When we act, we do this based on reasons and control our actions in light of the demands of being reasonable. So, for example, I might become particularly angry at a careless driver but, nevertheless, as a reasonable creature, control my anger and not swear endlessly at him.

In a section entitled "Self-mastery and moderation and their ultimate motivation" (D 109), Nietzsche argued that the situation is different. "Our"

> intellect is only the blind instrument of *another drive* which a *rival* of the drive.... While 'we' believe that we are complaining about the vehemence of a drive, at bottom it is one drive *which is complaining about another.*

The conflict is not between our rational self and our unruly drives. Rather, it is between drives, and though Nietzsche did not explicitly say so in this passage, our intellect is itself only an outgrowth of the drives. One drive might win out over the others, leading to the illusion that there is a simple "I" that is controlling the others, but that is an illusion.

A further feature of the traditional picture I mentioned above is that when we act, we do so intentionally. We *know* what we are *trying* to do. Fred may have failed to help Mabel feel better, but at least he tried because he knew what he was trying to achieve. Therefore, we find Fred worthy of moral praise since he intended, and so trying to do the right thing. But Nietzsche believed this to be a mistake. In a section entitled "The so-called 'ego,'" he noted that, though we may be conscious of "extreme" states like anger or hatred, there is little reason to think conscious states are the only aspects of our mind causing us to do things.

Furthermore, the fact that some states have conscious manifestations does not mean that they are what we think they are, or cause what we think they cause. Drives, which cause actions, operate below the level of consciousness. "*We are none of us* that which we appear to be in accordance with the states for which alone have consciousness and words, and consequently praise and blame" (D 115). Consciousness reveals only so much about the causes of our actions, and to think that it reveals *everything* about them is incorrect. But this is a "primal delusion," that "one knows, and knows quite precisely in every case, *how human action is brought about*." We *interpret* what we do, that is, try to make sense of what we do, but what actually causes our action, and the stories we tell ourselves about those causes can easily come apart. We are "unknown to ourselves."

3. The Demon and the Madman: *The Gay Science*

T he Gay Science (GS) is often seen as the opening of a different chapter in Nietzsche's thought since it introduces two of his most famous ideas–the Death of God and the Eternal Recurrence. We will discuss these ideas presently, but, as I emphasized in the previous chapter, it would be wrong to think there is some yawning chasm between *Daybreak* and *The Gay Science*. When Nietzsche began working on some of the material of *The Gay Science*, he was thinking of it as simply a continuation of *Daybreak*, and the first four books of GS were published only a year after the publication of *Daybreak*. On the other hand, on finishing those first four books, Nietzsche immediately turned to work on a very different work, *Thus Spoke Zarathustra* (Z). In a sense, he was already working on Z when writing the fourth book. Toward the end of GS, Nietzsche introduced the character of Zarathustra, the prophet of his philosophy; it is a section written in a style that intimates the curious character of Nietzsche's writing in *Thus Spoke Zarathustra*. So, while much of *The Gay Science* seems like it could easily be part of *Daybreak*, it contains pointers to the radically different *Zarathustra*. This might make one think that although there isn't a radical break between D and GS, there is a significant change with the publication of Z. That is right: Z is very different indeed. But after its publication, Nietzsche added a fifth book to the GS, entitled "We fearless ones," which seems to be more in tune with his later works, *Beyond Good and Evil* and *On the Genealogy of Morality* than with *Thus Spoke Zarathustra*; those books are much closer to *Daybreak* than they are to *Thus Spoke Zarathustra*. It is better, I think, not to see what is new in the GS as a major shift in Nietzsche's thought, but instead view the GS as a natural progression from

Daybreak through to *Beyond Good and Evil. Thus Spoke Zarathustra,* as we shall see, is the outlier in Nietzsche's writings.

Back to *The Gay Science,* first a word or two about the book's title. The "gay" or "joyful" science–*Die fröhliche Wissenschaft*–expresses Nietzsche's attitude to how one should conduct any systematic investigation. *Wissenschaft* is translated as "science," but the connotations of the German word are much broader than that of the English "science:" any systemic body of knowledge, including history, philosophy, philology, or whatever is a science in this sense. The "joyful" element to which the title alludes is more difficult to convey with any concision, but we shall begin with what Nietzsche says about the ancient Greeks in his preface to the second edition. The Greeks were, he claims, "superficial–*out of profundity!*" As always with Nietzsche, there is a lot packed into a tiny expression. Recall that in *The Birth of Tragedy,* Nietzsche admired the Greeks for their capacity to grasp the awful nature of reality and yet, at the same time, clothe it aesthetically so that reality could be born. The relation between knowledge, art, and existence remained a key theme for Nietzsche. The "Schopenhauer's question," namely, "does existence have any meaning?" still haunted him (GS 357). The Greeks learned to "stop bravely at the surface, the fold, the skin; to worship appearance, to believe in shapes, tones, words–in the whole Olympus of appearance." But this, Nietzsche suggested, is not timidity or cowardice, but born out of a recognition of the true nature of reality. For the Nietzsche of *The Gay Science*–and beyond–there is a deep need to pursue the sciences in good intellectual conscience. But in so doing, the aim is not truth for its own sake. Indeed, Nietzsche increasingly probed the idea that truth is an unconditional value, and, correspondingly, that we have a duty to pursue truth whatever the price. He was mainly concerned with the need for a way to affirm existence and, at the same time, recognize the truth regarding it. This implies recognizing the truth, and its terrible aspect, and somehow remaining joyful rather than resigned to pessimism. For the second, 1887, edition, Nietzsche added revised versions of some poems that he had previously

published in a journal, and subtitled the work "La *gaya* scu.
Ecce Homo, he explained that his use of this expression was inspn ∟
by "the Provençal concept ... [of the] unity of *singer, knight,* and *free spirit,*" a reference to the troubadour who composed and performed poetry, sometimes under the patronage of a local court or traveling. Nietzsche saw his "gay science" as promotion of honest artistry as a form of life.

> What if some day or night a demon were to steal into your loneliest loneliness and say to you: 'This life as you now live it and have lived it you will have to live once again and innumerable times again; and there will be nothing new in it, but every pain and every joy and every thought and sigh and everything unspeakably small or great in your life must return to you, all in the same succession and sequence....The eternal hourglass of existence is turned over and over again, and you with it, speck of dust!'

In this passage (GS 341), Nietzsche asked the reader to consider how one would react to such a demon. Would "you not throw yourself down and gnash your teeth and curse the demon?" Or would you experience a "tremendous moment" and answer to the demon, "You are a god, and never have I heard anything more divine"? This is Nietzsche's introduction of the concept of "eternal recurrence."

Nietzsche entitled this passage "the heaviest weight," suggesting that the thought of every detail of your life eternally recurring is a great psychological burden. Just where Nietzsche placed this passage in the GS is significant. It is immediately followed by the passage that introduces the character of Zarathustra, written in the poetic style of *Thus Spoke Zarathustra*. In *Ecce Homo*, Nietzsche begins his review of *Thus Spoke Zarathustra* by stating that the "basic idea" of that work is "the thought of the eternal return." So, to repeat a point I made above, GS presages *Thus Spoke Zarathustra*. But what is the "basic idea" of the eternal return? At first glance, it is remarkably simple. It seems to be a psychological test of whether one can affirm one's own life. Is your life such that you would welcome it occurring over and over again, without anything at all being different, or is it such that you view the prospect with terror? If you say yes, then you are happy with your life, if no, then you are unhappy. But things are far from being that simple.

First, it seems straightforward that we are being asked whether we can have either a positive or negative attitude toward the demon's proposition. Not as straightforward is what *kind* of attitudes are relevant here. Liking or not liking are too crude to capture the kinds of reaction that the demon's proposition is supposed to elicit. Elsewhere, Nietzsche gave us a clue to what kind of attitude he had in mind. This is a concept that he was thinking about at the same time as the eternal recurrence, and it is that of "*amor fati*" or "love of fate." In the first section of book 4 of *The Gay Science* (section 247), he wrote:

> I want to learn more and more how to see what is necessary in things as is what is beautiful in them—thus I will be one of those who make things beautiful. *Amor fati*: let that be my love from now on! ... [A]ll in all and on the whole: some day I want only to be a Yes-sayer!

Notice that there is love of *fate* and a recognition of what is "necessary" in things. So one might put matters this way: it is not merely that I accept that certain things were necessary for the good things to happen, such as, for example, going through the pain of a divorce, which leads to a new love. That would be not affirming one's life, but affirming only a *part* of it. For one could consistently recognize that the divorce was necessary, but nevertheless wish that it weren't so. Nietzsche, I think, didn't want us to merely affirm certain parts of our lives and begrudgingly recognize that some things were necessary for those parts. Instead, he wanted us to affirm—"say yes"—to life as a *whole*, rather than dividing it into parts to which one can "say yes" and those to which one does not make the same proclamation. It is to see and affirm everything as equally necessary. To affirm is not to see everything as good—that would be absurd—but to have an equally positive attitude to everything that enters into its composition. It is life as a whole that is affirmed. The thought of the eternal return is a test to see if one has the attitude of *amor fati*; whether, that is, one affirms life.

The eternal return might not be merely a test to discover those who do affirm life, but instead a device to get the reader to attempt to affirm. It doesn't simply find out who affirms but tries to encourage affirmation in the reader. But neither of these readings is quite right. For it is also, at the very least, a test to determine who *can* "affirm" rather than just an injunction to do so. Nietzsche asked whether or not one is capable of affirming, suggesting that some—perhaps very few—are capable of doing so, whereas many others are not. And in his notebooks, he suggested that it is slightly more than a test. It is "a doctrine.... powerful enough to work as a breeding agent: strengthening the strong, paralyzing and destructive for the world weary" (*The Will to Power* 862). When Nietzsche asked in GS 341, "how well disposed would you have to become to yourself to *long for nothing more fervently* than this ultimate confirmation and seal?" he was *encouraging* readers to *become* so well-disposed—something, he believed, that only the strong are capable of.

But there is a puzzle here too. For, in various places, Nietzsche seems to suggest that we are nothing but "pieces of fate:" everything that occurs to us is mere happenstance, and not caused by anything we *do*. Thus, in the section immediately after the introduction of the concept of *amor fati*, entitled "personal providence" (GS 276), he talked of everything turning out "for the best"—not because of some divine plan, but because of the "beautiful chaos of existence" which produces a "harmony" in the events that constitute a life and, crucially, a "harmony that sounds too good for us to dare take credit for it." One doesn't *do* anything to produce harmony; it just *occurs*. But *affirming* one's life sounds awfully like something one *does* and also, something that Nietzsche encourages us—or at least the strong among us—to do. So, if we cannot *do* anything to affirm, what is the point of trying to encourage a few persons to affirm? I propose to leave this issue until later in this chapter. I will also say a little more about the eternal recurrence in the next chapter. Right now, I shall turn to the second of Nietzsche's most famous ideas that are introduced in *The Gay Science*, namely the "death of God."

The death of God

Section 125 of the *Gay Science*, entitled "*The* Madman," is a brilliant example of Nietzsche's ability to pack into a relatively short piece of writing some profound, prophetic, and subtle ideas. In outline, it contains the following: a madman arrives at a marketplace in the bright morning light, and lights a lantern. He cries "incessantly" that he is "looking for God." Many of the people in the square don't believe in God, and so start to mock him, shouting over each other and laughing. Has God emigrated? Has he been lost? The madman stops them by giving his own answer to the question of where God has gone. "We have killed him ... We are all his murderers!" he exclaims. He then asks some questions about what this means for us. Now that we have "unchained the Earth," to where are we spinning, are we breathing empty space? Do we need to light lanterns in the morning rather than rely on the sun to rise? God is dead and what we smell is "divine decomposition." And is the magnitude of the deed too great for us? "Do we not have to become gods in order merely to appear worthy of it? he asks," adding that "whoever is born after us will on account of this deed belong to a higher history than all history up until now!" His mockers now become silently disconcerted, as the madman throws down his lantern, declaring that he has "come too early ... the tremendous event is still on its way" and, in fact, the deed done—the murder of God—is as remote as the stars to the people in the marketplace, even though the killing was done by them. The madman, it is reported, broke into churches, chanting "Grant unto God eternal rest," and when challenged, he stated that churches are nothing more than tombs of God's existence.

What are we to make of this story? The first thing to emphasize is that Nietzsche himself did not claim to have refuted God's existence. For the most part, he simply took atheism as the only viable intellectual position on this issue and did not attempt to argue for it. "What decides against Christianity now is our taste, not our reasons," he wrote (GS 132). Remember, after all, that the madman's announcement of God's death is directed at people who already do not believe in God. The passage is about the aftermath of the abandonment of that belief, but the crowd in the marketplace seems utterly unconcerned about how it will affect them. The madman is fervently exclaiming that this event will have a monumental impact, of which those in the marketplace have little or no inkling. The madman has come "too early" for the effect to have occurred.

Before we come to what that effect is, it is clear, I think, that the "madman" is Nietzsche himself. The madman has been trying to think through the consequences of God's death, recognizing that, metaphorically, the earth has now been unchained. The declaration that he has "come too early" reflects something Nietzsche says about his own work, namely that it is "untimely" and what is needed are philosophers and philosophies "of the future" (*Beyond Good and Evil* is subtitled "Prelude to a Philosophy of the Future"). In the preface to the *Anti-Christ*, Nietzsche wrote: "[m]y day won't come until the day after tomorrow. Some people are born posthumously." The reaction of those in the marketplace is reminiscent of a situation that Nietzsche described in GS 2. He counted himself as one of the few with a genuine intellectual conscience, finding contemptible those people who do not react to questions about existence, like himself, without hatred or at least faint amusement. There is faint amusement in the marketplace, not at the question so much, but at the person asking it, and that is because they have no real grasp of the question's enormity.

What of the lantern? Nietzsche had recently started to stay in Sils Maria, which he would revisit for three months almost every summer for the rest of his sane life. Despite his continuing poor health—his poor eyesight meant he could no longer read, and so he concentrated on writing, or, rather, dictating his own insights—the village in the Swiss Alps became a sanctuary for him. He stayed in a small room, lit by a single lantern. Nietzsche—the solitary man with a solitary lantern—confronted those not ready for his thought. There is, I think, further significance to the image of lighting the lantern in broad daylight. If God is light, and he is dead, then another source of light is required. This is obviously not the literal sense of darkness, just as it is not literally the case that the earth has become unchained. Rather, it suggests that God was supposed to be the source of meaning and value in our world. Nietzsche realized, and those in the marketplace did not, that the death of God means the decay—the "decomposition"—of that which has supported the meaning and values shaping the existence in the Judeo-Christian world. The lantern is a human-made source of light: it is humanity that will have to become the source of metaphorical light in the future.

This brings us to the significance of God's death for Nietzsche: its impact on the ideals, meanings, and values possible for human lives. Its content is far more subtle and complex than the simple thesis positing that without God, life becomes devoid of value. The first point is this: Nietzsche didn't think such values—and we will come to what these might be a little later—would simply disappear overnight. He had several reasons. First, he didn't seem to think Christianity would disappear altogether. He believed, quite plausibly, that people aren't Christians because they have some evidence for the existence of God, but rather because they are of certain psychological dispositions and live in certain cultures where that way of understanding humanity's place in the cosmos suits the needs of the human creature. No amount of rational criticism is going to shift the complex combination of culture and psychology that determines someone's Christianity. Instead, Nietzsche became increasingly concerned with its significance of the death of God for the small number capable of adequately appreciating it.

Second, Nietzsche believed that sincere atheism is only part of the story. I said above that the death of God is the death of that which underpins meaning and the values of the Judeo-Christian world. What that does *not* mean is that the values disappear overnight, or that it is inevitable that they disappear at all, even if we all became atheists overnight. What Nietzsche had in mind was the broader notion that Christianity provides an overarching account, or *interpretation*, of human existence and all that we experience within it. Our sufferings and misfortunes are not meaningless events, but instances of punishment, the taint of original sin, or part of an earthly testing ground, only to be redeemed in the afterlife. One's fortunes, advantages, and talents are not the mere caprice of nature, but gifts from God. Injustices on Earth will be corrected in heaven, and the meek shall inherit everything. The concatenation of events—which really is nothing other than the "beautiful chaos of existence"—is imbued with meaning and order, with reasons for why just such and such happens, and why what happens is the best. This interpretation of human nature, and the place of human beings in nature generally, also gives intelligibility to certain ideals of human life. We are all created equally in God's image, and the exemplar of a good life is Christ's selflessness in giving his life to redeem the world. Charity, compassion, selflessness, and concern for others represent the ideal human traits. The truly good people give themselves in the service of others and are not driven by the acquisition of worldly goods or pleasures.

The death of God is the death of this all-encompassing interpretation of human nature. But as I noted, its implications are complex. It does not, as I mentioned above, mean the values that disappear. And not only did Nietzsche think Christianity would remain alive for many people, but he also believed that the values of selflessness, which are structured by the ideals that the Christian account of human nature ascribes, remain even for atheists who explicitly reject Christianity. The most conspicuous example of this is Schopenhauer. He was a self-declared atheist, and yet at the same time professed an ethics of selflessness and compassion, along with an ascetic conception of virtue. The good person is one who chooses a life of voluntary poverty and chastity. Nietzsche, however, thought Schopenhauer had not properly reflected on the implications of his atheism. He had rejected the Christian interpretation of human existence but had not questioned the values that were shaped by it. This point is behind the first mention of the death of God in *The Gay Science*, which is entitled "New Battles" (GS 108): "God is dead; but ... there may be caves in which they show his shadow.–And we–we must defeat his shadow as well!" Schopenhauer's ethics–and, as Nietzsche foresaw, the morality of the liberal West–stood and still stands in the shadow of God.

Does this mean that we should simply reject the values that the Christian interpretation underwrites? Should Schopenhauer have dropped compassion as well as God? Again, matters are not that simple. Nietzsche's intention was not a total rejection of Christian values, but what he termed in later works the "re-valuation of all values." Rather than taking, say, compassion as *unquestionably* of positive, and ever overriding moral worth, we should consider its worth as we do other values, in light of the correct conception of human nature. That is when, as he put it in GS 109, "the shadows of god no longer darken us," and we "begin to naturalize humanity with a pure, newly discovered, newly redeemed nature." This requires a cold look at just what kind of creatures we are and the invention of new ideals for them. Nietzsche saw himself right at the beginning of this task: as such, he had come to the marketplace too early.

"Beautiful chaos of existence"

Nietzsche returned to the death of God once more in *The Gay Science*, right at the beginning of the fifth book. We shall return to it, but not in this chapter. As I mentioned above, the fifth book was written when Nietzsche was composing what are perhaps his two greatest works, *Beyond Good and Evil* and *On the Genealogy of Morality*. That is why I shall revisit his thoughts about God's death in the context of discussing his later works. But as well as the possibility of *revaluing* all values that come with it, there is a further thing that Nietzsche claimed in *The Gay Science*–namely, that values themselves are human creations. As I mentioned, we can think the madman lighting a lantern is an indication of "illumination"–of meaning and value–which is not from God but from human beings. In this connection, Nietzsche wrote in GS 301 of the "delusion of the contemplative ones." The delusion is that we are merely spectators, and that value is something that is there independently of us. Beauty is just "there, anyway." Instead, the world independent of human beings is completely devoid of value: "whatever has *value* in the present world has it not in itself, according to its nature–nature is always value-less–but rather has been given, granted value, and we are the givers and granters."

Now, the claim that value in the world–beauty, both aesthetic and moral–is (somehow) projected onto the world by human beings who feel and judge, was not new to Nietzsche. The great 18th-century Scottish philosopher, David Hume, said that we "gild and stain" natural objects with "colours borrowed from internal sentiment." Like Nietzsche, Hume thought that values (somehow) depend on our feelings for their existence. Nietzsche, however, didn't merely see this as a fact about values, but also as something that we need to be conscious of and exploit. We "misjudge our best power, and underestimate ourselves just a bit. We ... are neither as proud or as happy as we could be." Not only did Nietzsche suggest that values should be revalued, but also that we should further view ourselves as "creators" of value. More precisely, in later works, he called for "philosophers of the future" to be creators of value.

We will pursue that thought–and its relation to the project of "revaluation"–later in this book. But it is connected to another idea I mentioned earlier in this chapter: that one can read *The Gay Science* as promoting honest artistry as a form of life. There is the terrible question about the meaning of existence, to be met with a superficiality born from profundity. The "superficiality" is not supposed to license what we would normally construe as superficiality, but instead a concern with *forms*, of imposing, of creating something aesthetically pleasing out of the "beautiful chaos of existence." In some moods, Nietzsche seemed inclined to think that imposing artistic interpretations meant wilfully embracing an illusion. Thus, in GS 299, "What one should learn from artists," he wrote of viewing aspects of life in such contexts, so that "each partially distorts the new [view] one has of the others and allows for only perspectival glimpse." In GS 107, "Our ultimate gratitude to art," there is a mention of a "good will" to appearance, to art as the "cult of the untrue." This echoes *The Birth of Tragedy*, namely that "an aesthetic phenomenon is existence still bearable to us." In a much-discussed passage, entitled "One thing is needful!" (GS 290), Nietzsche suggested that we should treat ourselves as artworks. The one "needful thing" is

> [t]o "give style" to one's character—a great and rare art! It is practiced by those who survey all their strengths and weaknesses that their nature has to offer and fit them into an artistic plan until each appears as art and reason and even weakness delight the eye…. Here the ugly that could not be removed is concealed; there it is reinterpreted into sublimity…. In the end, when the work is complete, it becomes clear that how it was the force of a single taste that ruled and shaped everything great and small.

One should try to turn oneself into some art object, giving a formal unity to everything that constitutes oneself. But if this really is one thing that is "needful," how does it square with what we said about *amor fati*? That doctrine invited us to affirm everything about our life. Superficially, giving style to one's character seems to be motivated by a desire to *change* something about one's self, which seems at odds with *affirming* everything about one's life. One way to resolve this tension is to see the notion of "giving style to one's character" not as a matter of changing anything that constitutes yourself, but instead giving it an artistic *interpretation* of all the facts, be they good or bad, which jointly constitute one's self.

Nothing about *you* changes, except a shift in the attitudes one has toward those facts. This, in turn, will tell us a little more about what it is to "affirm" one's life. One can offer a pleasing interpretation of one's self and its interconnecting parts.

But a little reflection shows that this reconciliation of *amor fati* with giving style to one's character doesn't really work. One thing to note is when Nietzsche asked us to "affirm" things by wishing for their eternal recurrence, he prompted us to affirm not only facts about ourselves but every trivial fact, including "this spider and this moonlight between the trees" (GS 341). It is difficult to see how these facts can fit into an "artistic interpretation" of one's self. Second, in the passages about eternal recurrence, *amor fati*, and affirmation, the implication is that what we affirm involves fully recognizing that what one affirms is indeed something ugly, awful, or undesirable. It is facing up to the terrible truth and yet still affirming it. But in "giving style" to one's character, Nietzsche suggested that what we cannot remove, we must somehow conceal or at least make beautiful.

There is a further problem with the idea of giving style to one's character, a problem similar to the one I picked up on when discussing *amor fati*. The injunction to "give style to one's character" seems an injunction to *do* something. We should try to change, or at least artistically reinterpret, our character. But as I noted about *amor fati*, Nietzsche thought of us as "pieces of fate." Recall that for him, a person is nothing but a collection of different, interacting, drives. No agent or self stands above, and is in control of, drives; instead, there are competing drives, with some drives overcoming others. Just as I asked regarding affirmation, how could "I" be said to "do" anything called "affirming, in what sense could "I do" anything to give style to my character?

The beginnings of an answer are given a little later in a section entitled "Long live physics!" (GS 335). Its title might seem initially puzzling since this passage starts with a question about self-knowledge, a topic that seems a million miles away from physics. We think we have self-knowledge in the sense that we think we know directly what we are thinking, what we are intending to do, what we want, etc. We can just "tell" all that through our own consciousness. But this is, at best, a surface. Any judgments or intentions have "a prehistory in your drives, inclinations, aversions, experiences," none of which needs to be knowable through consciousness. What guides us in thought and action is not consciousness but "opinions, valuations, and tables"–drives–"most powerful levers in the machinery of our actions," which remain "unknowable" and "impenetrable." This claim prompted two thoughts for Nietzsche. First is that we should leave such "chatter" behind and not take our consciousness to reveal what causes us to act. Second, we should limit "ourselves to the purification of our opinions and value judgments and to the creation of tables of what is good that are new and all our own." Further, we want "to become who we are–human beings who are new, unique, incomparable, who give themselves laws, who create themselves!" This brings us back to the territory of "giving style to one's character," and in a way that seems to exacerbate the problem at hand: how one could do anything to give style to one's character when one is a "piece of fate." Here Nietzsche talked about human beings creating themselves, which seems an impossible feat. Surely, creation is not only something we do, hence raising the piece of fate problem, but we need to exist already to create "ourselves." To compound that puzzle, Nietzsche posited that we must "become who we are." If we "are" already, what sense is there to "becoming" what we already are?

I will postpone the discussion of "self-creation" and "becoming what one is" until a later chapter, focusing right now on the pieces of fate puzzle. Finally, in the section entitled "Long live physics!" Nietzsche got to physics. To achieve the goal of creation, we must "become … discovers of everything lawful and necessary in the world: we must become physicists … hitherto all valuations and ideals have been built of ignorance of physics or in contradiction to it." This suggests that changing ourselves–creating new values and giving style to our character–is not something we do directly. We do so by learning about ourselves as natural objects placed in an environment, subject to natural laws and causes; changes in ourselves—in our drives—must be affected in physical ways. Nietzsche often talked of physiology and diet as determining a person's values and behavior, and so changes in the person are physical. Given that consciousness doesn't reveal the drives to us, then to "survey all [one's] strengths and weaknesses" involves trying to figure out what one's drives are by considering one's history and environment rather than one's conscious thoughts. Still, one might say: "although I don't 'give style' to my character directly, but only doing so by trying to affect my most unconscious drives by changing the environment in which I am placed, am I still not *doing* something." The "pieces of fate" problem still seems to be there, as does the puzzling claims about "creating one's self" and "becoming what you are." The matter runs rather deep, and, as we shall see in later chapters, Nietzsche's radical view of ourselves runs just as deep.

4. Nietzsche's Bible: *Thus Spoke Zarathustra*

I n a letter to Paul Deussen from November 1888, Nietzsche wrote that *Thus Spoke Zarathustra* (Z) would be "the foremost book of the millennia, the bible of the future." No doubt Z is his most famous work, one, as I mentioned, which was distributed among German soldiers during World War I. Nietzsche referred to Z frequently in his subsequent writings, and devoted a lengthy discussion of it in *Ecce Homo*. The work was influential in countless ways. It inspired, for example, Richard Strauss's tone poem, *Also Sprach Zarathustra*, a piece of music now more associated with Stanley Kubrick's film *2001: A Space Odyssey* than it is with Nietzsche. Similarly, Gustav Mahler found musical inspiration in the work. It also fascinated Carl Gustav Jung, influencing his school of psychoanalysis. Paradoxically, Z influenced both the Nazi and the Zionist movement. It is sometimes described as "philosophical novel," not a bad description, but one that doesn't quite capture the florid nature of the prose, or the fact that much of it is a collection of speeches, sometimes shrill enough to test one's tolerance; it always ends with the triplet "Thus spoke Zarathustra" or, occasionally, musical mode–songs which also end with "Thus sang Zarathustra." It is replete with animal imagery, with different creatures standing as symbols for various aspects of human character traits. It is quite unlike any of Nietzsche's other works, and certainly, nothing like it exists in the canon of Western philosophy. Nietzsche himself variously conceived of it–not only as his "bible," but also as a "symphony" or as "poetry." The invocation of Zarathustra as its principal character, whose name derives from the Persian prophet of Zoroastrianism, obviously reinforces the religious connotations of the work.

Though Z is his most famous work, its centrality to philosophically-minded readers of Nietzsche has diminished.

Certainly, when serious Nietzsche scholarship was in its infancy in the English-speaking world, *Zarathustra* commanded the most attention. Walter Kauffman, a Princeton scholar to whom English-speaking scholarship owes a great debt, edited an influential collection of Nietzsche's works entitled *The Portable Nietzsche*, a volume that contained snippets from some of the philosopher's works and complete translations of only four of his books, one of which was *Thus Spoke Zarathustra* (the others being *Twilight of the Idols, The Antichrist* and *Nietzsche Contra Wagner*). It is exceedingly unlikely that a collection commissioned from a philosophically-minded editor these days would have this distribution of texts. At the very least, the *Genealogy*, perhaps Nietzsche's greatest work, would have to be included in its entirety, together with much more material from *Beyond Good and Evil, The Gay Science*, and *Daybreak* than Kaufmann provided. These works, though far from being dull and academic (in the bad sense of the word "academic"), contain far more subtle and nuanced presentations of Nietzsche's thought than the melodrama of *Zarathustra*. Z certainly engages and excites readers (and, one must add, also puts some readers off), but its success obscures his other works from which, philosophically speaking, there is more to be learned.

It was also written at a time of personal crisis for Nietzsche. The Lou Salomé affair completely devastated him. He felt Paul Reé had betrayed him, and drafted an abusive letter to him, as well as one to Reé's brother Georg, lambasting both Paul and Lou. Nietzsche's sister was herself sending abusive letters or, rather, one long letter to Reé's mother attacking both Paul and Lou. Now, according to Nietzsche's most recent and authoritative biographer, Julian Young, Nietzsche's volatile feelings towards Lou were also mixed with a suspicion of his sister's own motives. He began to think she was stoking his volatile feelings but only to get him to express Elisabeth's own resentment, rather than Nietzsche's ideal of love. But the whole affair and the intensity of his feelings for Lou and/or his suspicion of his sister left a mark on the views of women Nietzsche expressed in Z. Prior to the Salomé affair, Nietzsche's remarks on women had, or that period in history, been rather liberal. In Part I of Z, there is a section entitled "On little women, Old and Young," in which Nietzsche expressed some very different, and rather less palatable, thoughts about women. Zarathustra, for example, declares that women see men only as a means to children. Even the sweetest woman is bitter. The happiest man is one who wills; the happiest woman is one who obeys his will. Women are all so superficial; they are just shallow creatures of appearance. Most notoriously, the text contains the line, "You go to women? Don't forget the whip!" This line is often discussed in conjunction with a famous photograph of Nietzsche, Reé, and Salomé taken in 1882, which depicts Nietzsche and Reé in the place of horses on a cart, and Salomé inside the cart holding a whip. But since Salomé is holding the whip, it is very difficult to see what is the connection between the line in Z and the photograph. There is a consensus that the photograph is an allusion to Wagner's character Frika, who is represented in a carriage holding a whip while her husband is where the horse should be. None of this takes the sting out of what is said in Z about going to women with a whip. Nor does the fact that it is the old woman who says it to Zarathustra, rather than the other way around. It is difficult not to see such remarks as anything other than Nietzsche's bitterness at Lou and Elisabeth.

More on *Zarathustra*

Thus Spoke Zarathustra comprises a prologue and four parts. The first two parts were published in 1883, and the third in 1884. Part 4 was completed the next year, but only 45 copies were printed for private circulation, an inauspicious end to the writing of what would be his most famous work. I mentioned in the previous chapter that in *Ecce Homo*, Nietzsche stated that the "basic idea" of *Zarathustra* is "the thought of the eternal return." We shall come to that, but there is another connection to *The Gay Science*. If the madman of *The Gay*

Science is Nietzsche, so too is the character of Zarathustra. This is to say that Zarathustra is Nietzsche and the madman. Zarathustra descends from his solitude in the mountains, the same way Nietzsche came down to the marketplace from his room in Sils Maria. On the way, he encounters a saint, and Zarathustra is surprised to learn that the saint has yet to hear of the death of God. Like the madman, Zarathustra proclaims the death of God in the marketplace, but this time instead of his single lantern, Zarathustra claims a different source of illumination or meaning–the *Übermensch*. This is a term that used to be translated as "superman," but I will stick to the now commonly accepted "Overman" "I teach you the Overman," Zarathustra declares. But what is the "Overman?"

The first clue lies in the fact that when Zarathustra mentions the Overman, he also states that "man is something that should be overcome." The Overman is something that corrects some flaw or deficiency in human beings as they are now. What concerned the madman of *The Gay Science* was that the death of God leads inexorably to the loss of an overall meaning for, or interpretation of, human existence. The Overman is supposed to embody a new meaning for human existence. In an attempt to see what content that might have, let us work back from what Nietzsche took to be the flaw or deficiency in human nature that the Overman is supposed to overcome. This deficiency is exemplified by a figure Zarathustra refers to as "the last man," who is supposed to be the inevitable outcome of humanity without meaning, and who is "the most despicable figure." The last man is the inventor of "happiness," meaning a certain docile contentment and freedom from suffering. But this "happiness" is an aimless state of existence. "What is a star?" asks the last man. "What is creation? What is longing?" Without a guiding sense of purpose or meaning, humanity is reduced to the level of a herd of docile animals, avoiding discomfort. So, somehow, the Overman is supposed to offer an alternative interpretation of human existence. But how? It is not that the Overman preaches a substantial overarching meaning for human nature, as Christianity does. It is rather that the Overman is one that *possesses an aim* or *goal* which shapes and directs their lives, and that involves, necessarily, *discontentment* with circumstances and life. "I love," Zarathustra says, "the great despisers because they are great reverers and arrows of longing." It is not that there is a single meaning for every human being, but rather that there is something about human nature which means that humanity must have some aim or goal, and also must be discontented to be motivated to pursue it.

To understand what that might mean, we need to see what, in Nietzsche's view, made such a human being possible. In Part II of Z, in the section entitled "Of Self-Overcoming," Nietzsche introduced one of his most infamous doctrines, namely that of the "will to power." Human nature can be overcome, and so there can be overmen because human nature embodies this "will to power." To understand the Overman, then, we need to understand the will to power. Unfortunately, Nietzsche's treatment of the most famous doctrine in his most famous work is much too brief and metaphorical, and this is one of the many reasons Z is not philosophically rich. Zarathustra purports to offer us his insight into "life and the nature of all that lives," and that insight is the claim that all life consists in relations of "obeying" and "commanding." There is no basic "will to life," but where there is life, there is will to power. Zarathustra claims that this "secret life," i.e., the claim that behind all life are the relations of obeying and commanding, spoke to him. It said, "Behold! I am that which must always overcome itself." What are we to make of all this?

Recall that in Chapter 2, I introduced the notion of a "drive" briefly, and I said that Nietzsche's use of "drive," which he discussed in his unpublished notes, was inspired by the biology and psychology of his day. Taking "life" to be a biological category, Nietzsche's references to life can be understood as references to the drives that are the building blocks of living creatures, including human beings. Humans are compositions of drives, and drives are causal tendencies grounded in physiology. Drives are said to "aim" at things, and "value" things, but such language needn't be taken to mean that drives are conscious agents or human-like creatures. Instead, we can think of them as causal tendencies favored by natural selection. So, for example, one can say that trees grow tall because they want to reach the light as shorthand for a particular causal tendency that natural selection has favored, and which contributes to the flourishing of trees. Drives are causal tendencies which we may, therefore, speak of as "aiming" for things. But there is a further feature of Nietzsche's discussion of drives in his notebooks, which is directly relevant to our concerns. All drives exhibit the "will to power," he posited, adding that "every drive is a kind of lust for domination," involving "[a]ppropriation and incorporation, [which] is above all a willing to overwhelm, a forming, shaping and reshaping until the overwhelmed has gone completely over into the power of the attacker." Drives "command" and "obey" each other. Now, words "lust," "command," "obey," and, above all, "will," seem to reopen the worry that drives are nothing but tiny agents or people. But, again, this worry can be dispelled. We can understand that drive has a "lust for domination" in the sense that it is a causal tendency to produce its effect to a maximal degree, and will meet causal resistance from other drives. Since there is a conflict in the causal tendencies, there will be a "struggle" among drives. Think, for example, of weeds in a garden. They are compositions of drives, and the growth exhibits not merely the production of healthy plants, but also ones that sap all resources from, and smother, all other plants. The biological thesis prevalent when Nietzsche was writing, held that survival is not merely the result of adaption of the organism to its environment, but also the outcome of the *strength* of the causal dispositions placed in that environment. Weeds, for instance, "overcome" other plants. Inspired by this particular biological view, Nietzsche regarded all our drives to be tendencies to maximize their effects; that means that there will be causal resistances which those drives "seek to overcome." The "will to power" is not separate from the drives but a fact about the nature of all drives.

If human beings are collections of drives which tend to maximize their effects, drives that "seek to overcome" other causal resistances, we can piece together a picture of the "Overman" as someone who seeks to overcome himself or herself; since a person is a collection of drives, then overcoming one's self is overcoming one's drives. We also know that since a person is nothing but a collection of drives, then overcoming the drives comprising one's self will be a matter of one drive dominating or "overcoming" the rest of the drives. Without that, our drives can be such as to aim at different, incompatible goals, causing psychic disharmony. A single drive "dominating" all the other drives that comprise one's self is how one can understand "self-overcoming" and being an *Übermensch*.

If we return to Part I of Z, we can see this fitting with what Zarathustra preaches under the heading of "On the passions of pleasure and pain." There we are told that it is lucky to have only one "virtue" and that many people are a "battlefield" of virtues, where "each of your virtues is greedy for the highest. It wants your entire spirit, to be *its* herald; it wants your entire strength in rage, hatred and love." The English word "virtue" and its German equivalent *Tugend*, are significant because not only do they have a moral meaning—Mabel is a person of virtue—but the term also means *power* or capacity. A person's ethical character—her collection of "virtues," her patterns of loves, evaluations, plans, desires, etc.—is also her collection of powers or drives. Any such collection of virtues—in both senses of the term "virtue"—can be a battlefield because such virtues can push one in incompatible directions. So, for example, I might have a drive toward creating a masterful symphony and, at the same time, a drive towards achieving the status of Michelin-starred chef. Obviously, it is practically impossible to pursue both drives simultaneously: one simply must devote all the resources to one or the other in order to be successful, and a person unfortunate enough to possess these two drives would end up unsatisfied, either vacillating between two goals or remaining unfulfilled when one is sacrificed for the other.

A single dominant drive that can channel all one's other drives in a single direction is what Zarathustra preaches.

I have said that Nietzsche's conception of drives, and of the will to power, is inspired by the biology of his day. But in the example I gave, I talked about psychology rather than biology. The important thing to note is that while in Nietzsche's unpublished manuscripts, he considered biology as his model, his published works focus primarily on the psychology of human beings. Drives and the will to power are biological in inspiration, but in talking about morality, in particular in the published works, his focus was on their psychological manifestations. We shall see this when we discuss *On the Genealogy of Morality*. This means that the will to power has a psychological version too, and one which is important in understanding Nietzsche's views on morality. Each of us has aims, goals, desires, etc., for particular things. For example, one might have the desire to learn to play the guitar. How might that desire exhibit the "will to power?" One way to describe the desire—a way which *doesn't* exhibit the will to power—is as follows: I practice to achieve a certain proficiency and to play, say, three songs. I reach that level, and so my desire is met (or "satisfied" as philosophers put it). Though no one's desire to play the guitar may be actually like that, Nietzsche opined that most of our motivations are not like that. When I learn to play the guitar, I am continually motivated to improve my skill, precision, and command of the instrument. Of course, I may spend ages learning a particular song and be happy when I manage so to do, yet I do not rest content but seek to get better, more precise, and master more challenging material. My desire, though having the aim of playing the guitar, is not some finite goal like learning a particular song, but rather consists in the *activity* of mastering and overcoming greater and greater challenges. Any particular motivation, according to Nietzsche, exhibits will to power and has a particular goal—cooking an excellent meal, running a race, writing a book, cleaning the house. But as well as those goals, there is the particular way in which they are achieved—it is a matter of seeing them as challenges which we seek to gain mastery over. We want to make sure that the meal is just right and get more pleasure when the recipe involves something particularly difficult. And we don't rest there, but seek out even more difficult dishes to master.

The Overman then can be understood as an individual who has some all-encompassing drive or goal to which all his other drives are subordinate. But how can this be the "new meaning" to humanity? Nietzsche insisted, as mentioned before, that all value is a human creation. One way to understand this claim is that things are valuable *because* they are admired, sought after, and become the goal of human endeavor. They are not admired, sought after, and become the goal of human endeavor *because* they are valuable. Now, the Overman has a unified, overarching goal or aim, one which expresses his will to power. As he put it in *Twilight of the Idols*, Nietzsche's formula for "happiness" is "a yes, a no, a straight line, a *goal*" (Arrows and Epigrams, 44). Someone with an overarching drive for a single goal will thereby be a "creator of value." However, notice that this doesn't imply that there is *one single* goal for *every* human being. What is important is that the Overman pursues a single goal, but that goal can be different from person to person. The sense in which the Overman is the new meaning for humans is not that they create values and thereby "meanings," but because they are unified beings, whose drives are directed towards a single goal. Otherwise, human beings are "a ball of wild snakes that seldom have peace with each other" (Z, Part I). Indeed, a little later, Zarathustra intimates that since most of us are inchoate collections of competing drives, we are only fragmentary beings. I "walk among human beings as among the fragments and limbs of human beings" (Z Part I, "On redemption"). The Overman supposedly can offer a model of integration, which is also why Zarathustra "walk[s] among the fragments of the future."

The "last man"

But why, if Zarathustra "walks among the fragments of the future," does he foresee the coming of the "last men?" The problem seems particularly pressing if human motivations exhibit the will to power, namely a tendency to overcome—to achieve new goals—continually. The "last men" seem to *lack* precisely the will to power that Nietzsche thought of as an integral aspect of human motivation. How could that be so?

The "last man" is a vestige of the Christian interpretation of human existence, one where all suffering will be redeemed in the afterlife, and where the ideal of humanity is entirely selfless. We touched on this idea in the previous chapter, along with why the Death of God was a momentous event for Nietzsche: the decay of Christianity means the deterioration of what underwrites this interpretation of human existence. The vestigial aspect of this decaying interpretation of our nature is its moral component, in particular, the view that it is both possible and desirable to eliminate that suffering entirely, and concern for others is a morally central value. The danger in these (related) views is that they are precisely inimical to human nature. If human beings are essentially collections of drives that exhibit the will to power, then suffering is a necessary condition of our existence. In our activities, we not only encounter but also seek, resistances to overcome, and great effort to overcoming, which necessarily brings with it pain and sacrifice. Zarathustra implies that foregrounding suffering as something necessarily bad will encourage humans to seek easy comfort over the toil and pain of genuine creative endeavor. Not only that, but suffering and discontentment are an incitement to action and creative endeavor. Second, the ideal of selflessness—of promoting the needs and interests of others over one's own—is at odds with the nature of human creatures as constituted by drives that continuingly seek control and command over their objects. To put the matter crudely, creative endeavors can, at the very least, require one to ignore the needs of others in its pursuit. There are relatively benign examples of this idea. I might, for example, cancel my monthly charity payments to save money to study to be a chef. But this can tip into the less benign, where one can be coldly indifferent to the suffering of others and even exploit it. Stanley Kubrick was notoriously cruel to Shelley Duvall during the filming of *The Shining*, making her do the same scene repeatedly, not because he wanted to get the best take but because it increased her distress, making the character's discomfort more authentic. The scenes where the character is crying are, in many ways, as authentic as acting can be. Notice, furthermore, that this example relates to what we said about suffering: Kubrick was not only unconcerned about Duvall's suffering but actively sought to increase it. As Nietzsche put it in *Beyond Good and Evil* (225)

> You want, if possible (and no "if possible" is crazier!) to *abolish suffering*. And us? It looks as though *we* would prefer it to be heightened and made worse than it has ever been! Well-being as you understand it—that is no goal; it looks to us like an *end!*... The disciple of suffering, of *great* suffering—don't you know that this has been the sole cause of every enhancement in humanity so far?

We shall discuss in later chapters Nietzsche's worries about the general contours of Christian morality and also see that the morality Nietzsche thought of as inimical to humanity was itself a product of the will to power. There is a further worry about a central moral concept present in Z, namely that of pity and compassion. This is again a concern to be found in Nietzsche's other writings and better expressed in those than it is in Z, but we will begin with his dramatic presentation in Z. In Part II, Zarathustra meets on his travels a hunchback, "surrounded by cripples and beggars." The hunchback has heard of Zarathustra and tells him that people are having faith in him, but in order to prove himself and persuade the cripples, Zarathustra must cure them. Zarathustra refuses, saying, "If one takes the hump from the hunchback, one takes his spirit too—thus teach the people." Why does Zarathustra say this, and what does it have to do with pity?

Let us return briefly to the *Gay Science*, where pity is a particular concern, no doubt because of the pity's centrality in Schopenhauer's ethics, naming him in GS 99, and claiming that his words about compassion were "nonsense." Later on (GS 338), Nietzsche described compassion as a "religion of smug cosiness." Why did Nietzsche take such a dim attitude to compassion? He expressed a range of different criticisms of varying force. One early claim (GS 13) is that shows of compassion are really devices to elicit a feeling of power or superiority over others. Those who suffer are "easy prey," making us feel superior in comparison. No doubt that is true sometimes, but this observation alone is not particularly telling unless it could be valid for *all* instances of compassion. More telling is the complaint that underpins Nietzsche's characterization of pity as "smug cosiness" (GS 338). To feel compassion for another involves perceiving someone as suffering in some manner. But determining whether someone is genuinely suffering is not always an easy matter. If you see someone cut their hand badly and start writhing in agony, then it is clear that they are suffering. But most of the time, things are more complicated. What of the parent of a terminally ill child, or the person in an unequal marriage? One's immediate response might be "isn't that terrible," but in so doing one might be betraying not only a tendency to respond without a proper understanding of their situation, but also a view of how the features of their lives deemed to be misfortunes are conceived of by those who are the object of your compassion. The person showing compassion "knows nothing of the whole inner sequence and inner connection," determining the "misfortune" that is the object of compassion. Instead, compassion is superficial and "strips" from the person what is truly personal to him or her. This brings us back to the hunchback. His identity is partly determined by his physical condition, which not only constitutes a resistance to overcome—hence allowing the exercise of the will to power—but also shapes his character. His character is the product of the "whole inner sequence and inner connection," of which his hunchback is a decisive part. Thus, if "one takes the hump from the hunchback, one takes his spirit too." People are not merely superficial in their assessment of whether someone needs compassion. It is rather that the superficiality reflects a disposition to stay within a narrow circle of moral considerations. There are things, from your own perspective, that you consider the causes of suffering, and you stay within that circle and think better of yourself through your concern. You "want to help—but only those whose distress you properly understand because they share with you one suffering and one hope ... and only in the way you help yourself."

The Eternal Return

A prominent theme in Z is Zarathustra's great disgust (Ekel) at the world as he finds it, a world in the grip of a certain kind of morality. This fact conceals irony behind Nietzsche's choice of Zarathustra as his protagonist. Zarathustra—or Zoroaster—was a Persian prophet who saw the universe has fundamentally divided into two mutually exclusive categories, good and evil. Zarathustra is, therefore, one of the earliest teachers of a position that Nietzsche thought should be rejected, and so it is Zarathustra who is correcting his own mistakes. Nietzsche's next book, Beyond Good and Evil, is precisely an attempt to reject this fundamental division. Suffering and many other "evils" are not to be conceived as exclusively bad. But if Zarathustra is disgusted at the world, what are we to make of Nietzsche's eponymous work's "basic idea"—namely the eternal recurrence? It does not make an appearance in that work until Part III, in the section entitled "On the Vision and the Riddle." Its presentation is rather complex. Zarathustra is on a ship and recounts to the sailors aboard a vision he had, in which a riddle is contained. In this vision, he is climbing a mountain, carrying on his shoulder a half-dwarf, half mole creature; as Zarathustra begins to feel oppressed, he suddenly resolves to be courageous. At the top of the mountain, he sees the abyss but claims that courage can conquer it. The abyss represents both life and death, seen from Zarathustra's vertiginous position. "Was that *life?*" he muses—"Well then! One more time!" The dwarf jumps down, they discuss two eternal paths, and the dwarf claims that the paths are not straight. Instead, the paths are circular, and we are destined to walk them over and over again. Zarathustra, who is seized with fear at this thought, hears dogs bark in the background, and suddenly sees a shepherd, writhing and fighting a thick black snake hanging from his mouth. Now, Zarathustra's initial reaction to this sight is a potent mixture of dread, hatred, nausea, and pity. After trying unsuccessfully to remove the snake from the shepherd's throat, he screams out, "Bite down, bite down!" Having recounted this vision to sailors, he turns to them to ask what it means. They do not give him an answer. Zarathustra continues, telling them that the shepherd, heeding his advice, bites down on the snake, spits out his body, and stands as something "no longer human—a transformed, illuminated being."

On the one hand, it is relatively easy to see how the snake represents the dread, nausea and pity, and that the shepherd, rather than fighting off those feelings, absorbs them. It is also not implausible to see this scenario as representing a certain temptation—just as the snake of the Old Testament represents temptation—sitting with the idea that Z was Nietzsche's "bible." The temptation, in this case, is to give in to the dread, nausea and pity, to succumb to suicidal nihilism. That, of course, is resisted—the snake is killed, and the human is transformed into something else, the "radiant" and "laughing" Overman. But on the other hand, the elaborate setup and its outcome do not help convey the central point of the Eternal Return in the pithy way that GS, 341 does; nor does it give any hints about how the metaphor of biting the snake is supposed to show what it is to affirm the Eternal Return, thus becoming something more than human. It is nevertheless clear that at this stage of Nietzsche's thinking, the Eternal Return is a central concern of his, even though *what* it is supposed to mean is hardly transparent from the pages of Z. At roughly the same time as the composition of that work, Nietzsche's notebooks show that he was toying with the idea that the universe is offering the possibility of the eternal return. We will live the same life, in all its detail, repeated eternally. This is the "cosmological" reading of the Eternal Return. However, whatever enthusiasm Nietzsche might have had for his proof of the Eternal Return—and it seems that it was part of the metaphysical project that he abandoned but which his sister published as *The Will to Power*—the alleged *truth* of the Eternal Return doesn't seem relevant when it is presented in both *The Gay Science* and *Thus Spoke Zarathustra*. It is not presented as something true; instead, it is portrayed as a hypothetical situation, asking the reader to consider how they would react to that situation.

There is, however, another way in which the Eternal Return is significant, and that lies in its contrast with Christianity. In Christian doctrine, life on this earth, along with all the sufferings and misfortunes, are terrible but finite. There is a promise of an eternal life where sin is sloughed off, innocence restored, and wherein suffering is compensated. This story gives an overall interpretation of or meaning to human existence, particularly suffering. It is finite and redeemed in the afterlife, and all events fit into an overall plan. The doctrine of the Eternal Return is in stark contrast to this particular interpretation of human existence, the meaning of suffering, and the events that constitute worldly existence. There is no final meaning to suffering—one isn't suffering because of some plan—nor is it redeemed in another world. Life is not merely a precursor to a much better, eternal state. All that there is to one's existence is precisely *this* world, this sequence of events, and so it has to have significance solely on its own terms. Viewed in this way, the Eternal Return stands in stark contrast with the Christian meaning of human existence. But Z does not make it clear just what is the positive message of the Eternal Return.

Part IV of Z sees Zarathustra meeting characters and creatures that represent various things. There is a magician who seems to be

Nietzsche's idealization of Wagner, a man who is attaching leeches to his arm to suck away all his prejudice, two kings who are disillusioned with ordinary society, the last pope who is mourning God's death, the man who killed God (the "ugliest" man), and a beggar who voluntarily gave up all his riches. At the same time, Zarathustra is pursued by his own shadow. He invites all whom he meets to his cave. In one way, the people he met and gathered in his cave have understood part of Zarathustra's teaching, like, for example, the death of God. But they are not yet overmen, partly because they are followers, in this case, followers of Zarathustra himself. They are "higher" types because they are capable of breaking free of Christian meanings of human existence, but have not yet "overcome" themselves, for their valuations are still linked to the old ideal.

Various other things occur in the subsequent text, but there is an air of mockery, lightness, and expressions of joy. Zarathustra's guests are encouraged to dance, and there is a drunken song, wherein the Eternal Return is celebrated and affirmed. Zarathustra orchestrates an "ass festival," a Christian appropriation of a medieval pagan feast, but where the buffoonish nature of humanity is celebrated. These antics and the general levity of Part IV sets it apart from the rest of the work and can seem jarring. Some commentators, quite plausibly, see it as Nietzsche's attempt to express the Dionysiac in his philosophy—the wild, celebratory side of life. But, at least to my taste, the whole thing reads somewhat false and falls flat; fortunately, Nietzsche's subsequent writings are more serious in tone.

uth, Selves and the Truth about Selves: *Beyond Good and Evil*

I mentioned in Chapter 3 that the fifth book of *The Gay Science* seems to fit in best with the two works published after *Thus Spoke Zarathustra*, namely *Beyond Good and Evil* (BGE) and *On the Genealogy of Morality* (GM). This is true in a pedestrian sense, namely, that the fifth book was published a year after BGE and in the same year as GM. But, more importantly, some of its key content fits well with BGE and GM. It opens with a restatement of the Death of God, but one that is redolent with possibility and optimism. The next section of the book—to which we shall return in the context of discussing the GM—examines the relationship between the high value placed on truth on the one hand, and Christian morality on the other, a key theme *in* GM's third essay. The following section takes morality as a problem and, among other things, suggests that a *history* of morality is required to reassess the value of morality. This is precisely what GM offers. This list of themes from GS book 5 could continue, though I would not like the reader to go away with the impression that there is nothing in the fifth book of GS that isn't in either BGE or GM: there is plenty that is unique to it. But I shall occasionally refer to some materials in this book in this and the next chapter.

Beyond Good and Evil

Like many of Nietzsche's works, BGE touches on many subjects. Part 8, "Peoples and fatherlands," discusses various conceptions about national character in insightful, and often very funny, ways (he is particularly amusing about the English). Part 4, "Epigrams and entr'actes," is Nietzsche at his most "aphoristic" (the French "entr'actes" or "between the acts" is not, therefore, surprising). This part comprises many, often single-sentence, observations. Some, unfortunately, reflect his nastiness about women—animosity that was born of his disappointment with Lou Salomé ("Where neither love nor hate are in play, woman is a mediocre player" (BGE 115)). Some express philosophical theses: BGE 117 states that the "will to overcome an affect is, in the end, itself only the will of another, of several other, affects." Others seem to embody practical wisdom: "Sensuality often hurries the growth of love so that the root stays weak and is easy to tear up" (BGE 120). Part 6, "We scholars," discusses philosophy and philosophers—old, present and those of the future capable of creating values.

There is much more information in the BGE, which we do not have space to mention, let alone discuss. It is a book, as I said, that touches on almost everything. But what lies behind the title *Beyond Good and Evil*? As is usual with Nietzsche, things are not immediately evident from the work's preface, its opening sections, or, indeed, from his own account of BGE in *Ecce Homo*. It is not really until the final part of the work—Part 9, "What is noble?"—that an answer is forthcoming to what it might mean to go "beyond good and evil." Now, Nietzsche described himself as an "immoralist" in BGE, and because he did so, it would be easy to form the superficial impression that going "beyond good and evil" means the abandonment of morality, leaving a world without values. But it would be a total mistake to interpret going "beyond good and evil" and "immoralism" in that way. One reason for this error is the assumption that morality is a single thing (or that there is a single morality), either to be embraced or abandoned. A key motif of the central Part 5 of BGE, "On the natural history of morals," is that we—philosophers and ordinary people—are blind to the fact that there are many types of morality, and that the one which predominates today is only one of many, even though it seems to present itself as the only possible option. As Nietzsche put in BGE 202, modern morality "stubbornly and ruthlessly declares 'I am morality itself and nothing else is moral!'" In GM, Nietzsche will try to show that our present morality both differs from, and emerges from, another morality. Our present morality turns on a contrast between good and evil (böse), which differs from an earlier morality, which turns on a contrast between good and bad (schlecht). To go "beyond good and evil" is to go beyond the morality we now inhabit.

The good/evil and good/bad moralities are discussed in BGE 260, which will form the basis of his subsequent discussion in GM. The distinction between this contrast is closely related to another important distinction in Nietzsche, namely the distinction between "master" and "slave" moralities. Very roughly, Nietzsche argued that the morality marked by the good and bad contrast was–and is–viable. What is good is marked by fortune. A noble birth, confidence, independence, a person full of power and strength, and a set of honor relations that hold only between equals. Actions are called "good" only secondarily, things that are done by noble people. Those who live in accordance with "master" morality resemble the Overman mentioned in the previous chapter in the sense that they express a unity of purpose and relative indifference to others. They set their own goals and pursue them single-mindedly, expressing a unitary direction to their drives. The contrasting term "bad" applies to the masses of persons who are not so fortunate. The German word "schlecht" here means base or lowborn. These people are the sick, the timid, the poor, the ugly, the conquered, and the dispossessed. They cannot acquire what they want, they are weak, and not merely in the physical sense, but in the psychological one as well: they are timid, self-doubting, needing the comfort of others. The elites are the superior types, and the lowly ones are those who fail to have all the naturally good things on earth, like power, health, etc. This, to Nietzsche, was the "rank order of values" of the ancient world of the Greeks and Romans. But this morality has been displaced by a morality marked by a contrast between good and evil. What is previously thought of as bad–weakness, poverty, and so forth—is somehow interpreted as morally praiseworthy. The key concept here is that the morally good person is one who is essentially *selfless*—giving of himself or herself to others, not taking one's self to be better or more valuable than others, which is the opposite of the noble who pursues goals with at the very least an indifference toward other human beings. Furthermore, the fiction of free will as being able to do otherwise is added. The "masters" are not only terrible at what they do but also terrible because they could have chosen to do otherwise. To "go beyond good and evil" is to go beyond this morality, but not to go beyond a contrast between good and bad. Human beings are essentially evaluating creatures and cannot live without values.

We shall return to this when we get to GM, where Nietzsche gave his best articulation of this contrast between two moralities. Now let us turn instead to the very beginning of BGE. The preface begins strangely: "Suppose that truth is a woman—and why not?" The first section of Part 1 asks two questions about truth, namely, why pursue the truth in the way that we do, and what is the value of this will. "Granted we will truth: *why not untruth* instead?" These questions open the discussion of Part 1, entitled "Of the prejudices of philosophers," which comprises 23 sections critiquing various philosophical positions. This is the densest and most complicated sequence of writings in Nietzsche's entire corpus. It is followed by Part 2, "The free spirit," but the division between the two parts seem somewhat artificial because many of the topics of Part 1 are revisited in Part 2. It is impossible to convey much sense of the complications that lurk below the surface here, so I can only provide a tiny taste of its themes.

Nietzsche's claimed that most philosophy doesn't know how to approach the truth. When truth is supposed to be a woman, it should be understood as the idea that philosophy's approach is dogmatic. Its investigations start with some stubborn preconceived conceptions of what the world must be like and fail to question those presuppositions. Philosophy's advances are "clumsy" and have been "spurned," he posited. These presuppositions are not, as philosophers pretend to themselves, timeless insights into the nature of reality, but instead a "seduction of grammar or an over-eager generalization from facts that are really very local, very personal, very human all too human." Indeed, Nietzsche believed that philosophical systems are not the result of a disinterested pursuit of the truth, but expressions of the particular drives that the philosopher possesses. Every "great philosophy so far has been: a confession of faith on the part of its author, and a type of involuntary and unself-conscious memoir" (BGE 6). The great philosophical systems, those of Plato or Kant to choose two very famous examples, are, Nietzsche suggested, expressions of the kinds of drives and interests that constitute those individuals, and particularly the sets of drives comprising their moral outlooks. Their philosophical systems, which are purportedly objective descriptions of reality, are, in fact, conceptions of the world that best suit the moral inclinations of their inventors. Kant, for example, believed in a morality where ultimate responsibility rests on the spontaneous free choices of individuals, and his metaphysics reflected this moral belief: there is a second world where our will is free and unconstrained.

But what makes Nietzsche's philosophy different? Why is his philosophy not merely a reflection of the "order of the rank the innermost drives of his nature are placed relative to each other" (BGE 6)? Isn't Nietzsche's philosophy just an expression of his own drives? Nietzsche himself was aware of this danger, and attempted to guard against it by pointing to a difference between his philosophy and the other philosophies encapsulated in the final sentence of Part 1. "[F]rom now on, psychology is again the path to the fundamental problems" (BGE 23). His approach to philosophy was not to try to build a metaphysical system, but instead to understand human beliefs and behavior, including those of philosophical system builders. This is an aspect of what I referred to in Chapter 2 as Nietzsche's "naturalistic" philosophy. His approach is oriented around a theory of the nature of human beings, a theory built on empirical observation informed by the sciences of the day.

It is part and parcel of his project to "translate humanity back into nature" (*BGE* 230). The metaphysical pictures of nature, and our place in nature need to be replaced. We need to "gain control of the many vain and fanciful interpretations and incidental meanings that have been scribbled and drawn over that eternal basic text of *homo natura* so far." Humans have false conceptions about just what kinds of things they are, false conceptions that both philosophy and Christianity have invented and perpetuated.

Truth and Perspectives

As we have noted, Nietzsche opened the preface with a question about truth, also mentioning something he referred to as "perspectivism." This is a term that has become strongly associated with Nietzsche, so it is an appropriate place to discuss it.

One—thoroughly mistaken—view is to say that when Nietzsche talked about "perspectives," he meant to suggest that there is no such thing as truth. This idea has some textual backing. As I mentioned in the Preface, in an early unpublished essay, Nietzsche wrote that truth is a "mobile army of metaphors, metonyms … illusions that are no longer remembered as being illusions." During the early part of his career, he thought our beliefs are "falsifications"—beliefs that somehow involve distortions, and so are false. He did eventually abandon this claim, and I will explain why. Nietzsche insisted that *knowing* is from "a perspective." Knowing something is not the same as something being true, since there can be lots of truths we don't know—for instance, nobody knows whether there is an odd or even number of blades of grass in the world, but there is a fact of the matter—though what we do know must be true. But what does it mean to say that all-knowing is from a perspective?

Let us begin by thinking of a visual perspective. Anything we see is seen from a particular point of view, and, because of this, one's view of anything is only ever partial. I am sitting at my laptop, but I only see part of it. If I change my position, I adopt another perspective and see a different part of the computer. I then move again, and again, until I have a total view of it. All that seems straightforward, but Nietzsche believed everything is known or viewed from a perspective. Why? This is a little complicated, but I hope the following sketch will bring some clarity. When we know something, we are correctly representing the world to be a certain way.[1] Consider a map: it is a representation of a certain area. But what do we include in that map? Well, it depends on what one's interests or needs might be. If one is interested in camping, such a map will depict flat areas, footpaths, water features, etc. Other things that are not germane to hiking, like the location of guitar shops, for example, will be left out. If one's interests lie in architecture, then the map would show architectural landmarks, leaving out hiking features. Thus, a map can be an accurate representation but a *partial* or *selective* one. It is a representation of something from the *perspective* of certain kinds of interests. If we included every interest, the map would be complete, but such a representation is impossible.

Maps are, of course, human inventions. But all creatures operate with representations. A frog, for example, can represent a fly in its environment, so it can catch it. But its set of representations—its map—will be a very limited or partial one, one geared solely to its environment. The difference between quartz and granite makes no difference to the frog, and so it is not something that is represented from the frog's perspective. Instead, and to simplify somewhat, the frog carves up the world into "flies" and "not flies." Human beings, too, are natural creatures—that is, of course, a central plank of Nietzsche's naturalism—and so our representations are geared to our environment. We form a concept of fruit, for example, partly

1. More things are required than this, but we won't go into this issue here.

because doing so crucially contributes to our survival. That, though, is not a concept that the frog forms. All the ways in which we "carve up the world"–that is to say, organize what we experience and represent it–are from the perspective of our needs and interests.

Such thoughts are articulated in *The Gay Science*, and with them, the claim that our beliefs–our representations of how the world is–"falsify." Why did Nietzsche think that they do so? Well, one might suppose that carving up the world into categories like "fruit" or "fly" doesn't show us how the world "really is." This will either be revealed by science or remain hidden from experience. But it is highly unlikely that how creatures geared to their local environment organize experience reflect the world as it really is. If the world is "really" a collection of atoms, then even though it is useful for us to think in terms of trees and fruit because those beliefs are helpful in survival, they are really "falsifications" because "really" there are no trees or pieces of fruit. That is just the way *we* organize experience. "Life is no argument," as Nietzsche wrote in GS 121. And it is not only beliefs about fruit and trees that Nietzsche thought of as products of evolution and therefore likely to falsify. He held that this was the case even with our very fundamental concepts that figure in that vast majority of our beliefs:

> Through immense periods of time, the intellect produced nothing but errors; some of them turned out to be useful and species-preserving ... such erroneous articles of faith, which we passed on by inheritance, further and further, and finally became part of the basic endowment of the species, are for example: that there are enduring things; that there are identical things; that there are things, kinds of material bodies, that a thing is what it appears to be (GS 110)

Notice that this claim even spills into science. I mentioned above that we might think there are only atoms, but Nietzsche was skeptical of that claim, believing that even the concept of a "thing" is just a human construct. It is likely that *none* of our representations fits the world. The world is completely unknowable, and everything we think or say is a "falsification."

Nietzsche's later works do not, however, contain the claim that our beliefs falsify the world. He wrote straightforwardly about things being true and things being false. The most plausible reason for this as follows: Nietzsche, when he thought most of our beliefs were false, was thinking that our evolved beliefs falsify reality because of an assumed contrast with one *true* representation of the world, one that is free from perspective. But he came to realize that the idea of a representation of a world from no perspective (a "view from nowhere," to use the American philosopher Thomas Nagel's expression) is simply impossible. All representation is *from* a point of view. So, the "true world"—the one supposedly revealed from the view from nowhere—is a myth because there can be no such view from nowhere. Where does that leave our ordinary beliefs? Well, there is no reason to suppose they are false. It is a fact that there are trees and there is fruit. Sometimes we are wrong in a perfectly ordinary sense—I thought there was an apple, but it is really a wax replica—but there is no sense in saying that there is really no such thing as fruit, or indeed there is really no such thing as "things." Our daily perspective reveals a world containing fruit and trees, whereas a different perspective, say one of physics, reveals a world containing atoms. These two worlds are not in conflict with each other, and both reveal truths about the very same world. In the *Twilight of the Idols*, in a section entitled "How the true world became a fable" Nietzsche expressed a "history of an error," a sequence of views on the "true world." The earlier views describe a gap between the "true world"—how it really is—and a merely "apparent" one. His *Gay Science* view that we falsify reality certainly counts a philosophy that embodies such a contrast. There is a "true world," but our beliefs and thoughts, because they are perspectival, are false, and so the world we live in is just appearance. But in eliminating the idea that there is a view from nowhere revealing the "true world," we also get rid of the idea that the world which we experience is mere appearance. Thus, if we "have abolished the real world, what world is left? The apparent world perhaps ... But no! *with the real world, we have also abolished the apparent one!*"

This still leaves knowing as perspectival. Nietzsche also thought that being "objective" is perspectival as well. The most discussed passage of Nietzsche's work in relation to this view, and indeed with perspectivism in general, comes not from BGE but from *On the Genealogy of Morality*, but it seems appropriate to discuss it here since we are dealing with the topic. In GM III:12, Nietzsche warned us to guard against the myth of a "pure, will-less, painless, timeless, subject of knowledge," one of "pure reason." This is an allusion to Schopenhauer, who thought we grasp the universe from an objective standpoint when we disengage all our desires and emotions and become something like a passive mirror that simply reflects how things really are. Being "subjective," by contrast, is partly determined by our emotions, interests or desires, because these, at best, lead only to a partial view of the world and, at worst, can distort our view of the world. So, for example, my great love of a particular city might cause me to overlook its faults, downplay its shortcomings, and prevent me from properly appreciating the virtues of another city. So, to avoid the distortion of interests, emotions, passions, etc., we should aspire to a view that completely leaves these out: we should become passive so that the world as it really is merely impresses upon our "pure reason." Nietzsche, however, posited that this is a "myth" and suggested that instead of discounting our interests or affects, we approach objectivity by multiplying them. The "*more affects* we allow to speak about a matter, *the more eyes*, different eyes we know how to bring to bear on one and the same matter, that much more complete will our 'concept' of this matter." How so?

Recall what we have said about "perspective" and knowing. Our representations of the world come necessarily from our perspectives, interests, and concerns. Thus, as Nietzsche said in GM III.12, there "is *only* a perspectival seeing, only a perspectival 'knowing.'" Now, remember too what I said above about the map analogy. One set of interests, that of camping, made salient features relative to that interest. In doing so, however, it is selective and leaves out other things that are only salient from a different perspective. Again, my great love of some city might make only good things uppermost in my mind and make me blind to its faults. To get a richer and more informed view of the relevant matter–a more objective conception of it–one should introduce other interests that make other features more salient. So, for example, someone from a different city might introduce their own love of their city, and the comparison of perspectives helps us arrive at a more complete picture of our respective cities. Of course, that requires recognizing that sometimes our perspectives are distorted, but that is far from saying that objectivity is achieved by simply abandoning interests, loves, and desires. A more complete picture emerges only from a comparison of many perspectives and not the mythical view from nowhere.

More ideas from *BGE*

One key metaphysical belief that Nietzsche discussed in BGE, and which in the Preface he blamed on Plato, is the notion of "pure spirit" or, as he put it in BGE 12, "atomism of the soul." As I have mentioned in several places, Nietzsche's view is that there is not a single thing that is the self but, instead, we are collections of drives. He suggested that the "soul hypothesis" should be replaced with the "soul as a society constructed out of drives and affects" (BGE 12). He also continued with his skepticism about free will, again another topic we have already discussed in this book. BGE adds further criticism of the idea that we are responsible for our actions, a notion that is worth pausing over.

Suppose, for example, that what I do is determined by the kind of person I am. I am brought up in a certain culture, so the kinds of decisions I make are determined by that fact. I am, say, a person who values study and quiet, a fact about me that is shaped by my upbringing. In Nietzsche's language, I am a person who has drives to study and to quiet, drives that I have inherited, and which have been conditioned by my environment. Now suppose I do something that expresses one of my drives. I sit writing this chapter. Am I responsible for that action? Well, one might think not, because although the action expresses one of my drives, I didn't *choose* to have that drive. It is just something I "have," not because I wanted it, but it is part of the package that constitutes me, like my eye color and my height. But, the thought continues, I cannot be held responsible for an action stemming from a drive I didn't choose to have. To see this, imagine that overnight someone tinkers with my brain, and gives me a new drive, the drive, say, to tickle people. I then go around tickling people, who, rightly, complain about my intrusive behavior. Suppose, however, it is discovered that this drive was implanted in me the night before. I bet people would think that I was not responsible for what I did. Poor Kail had a drive he didn't want implanted in his head! He didn't agree to have this drive planted in him, and so we can't really blame him. But if this is so, one wonders what the difference is between having a drive implanted and one that a person is simply born with? It seems that I am only truly responsible for what I do if I choose the drives that constitute who I am. That is tantamount to creating yourself, being self-caused, or "*causa sui*" in the Latin expression. This, Nietzsche contended in BGE 21, is "the best self-contradiction" ever conceived in philosophy, a "type of logical rape and abomination." The longing for freedom of the will—and here Nietzsche surely thought in terms of responsibility—brings with it, though unwittingly, the impossible aspiration "of pulling yourself by the hair from the swamp of nothingness into existence."

These criticisms of Nietzsche's regarding the very conditions of responsibility and the impossibility of bringing oneself into existence seem to me to be serious ones, but also serve as a reminder of a problem we noted in the chapter of this book on *The Gay Science*. There, Nietzsche claimed that the "needful thing" is, somehow, to "give style to our character," and that this notion is sometimes framed as "self-creation." What was said there is not quite the same thing as bringing one's self into existence out of nothingness—Nietzsche of *The Gay Science* didn't suggest that—but it is related in the following sense: The worry about "self-creation" was that the very expression suggested that we *do* something to change our drives in order to become a "stylish" self, but if we are just collections of drives then we are just "pieces of fate." It looks as if we never really "do" anything. This, I suggested, is also connected to freedom of the will: if we are merely collections of drives, and have no center that is the "agent," then it is nonsensical to think that we can ever act freely.

These are complicated issues, and Nietzsche scholars vehemently disagree about the best way to resolve them (if, indeed, they can be resolved at all). Let me suggest a way to bring these threads together, one based on several thoughts from different scholars. Remember that the self is a collection of drives. In BGE, it is important to notice not only that collections of drives are just heaps but also that the drives stand in certain kinds of relations, and in particular, in relations of "commanding" and "obeying." For Nietzsche, this relation of commanding and obeying was also connected to "freedom of the will." He noted that "What is called 'freedom of the will' is the affect of superiority," a feeling that something has followed from what the drive "wants:"

> [T]he one who wills takes his feeling of pleasure as commander, and adds to it the feelings of pleasure from the successful instruments that carry out the task, as well as from the useful "under-wills" or under-souls—our body, after all, is only a society constructed out of many souls. (BGE 19)

Here Nietzsche was talking about relations between *drives*, and so none of this talk about "commanding" or "souls" should be taken to commit the homunculus fallacy. Drives "command" when they cause things to happen and overcome resistance, i.e., when other causal powers "obey"—that is, become directed towards the same "goal" as the "commanding" drive. So, for example, I have a drive to eat, and that drive commands various aspects of my body (which are drives) so that my body chews and ingests food. When it comes to "free will," BGE 19 seems to suggest that being "free" is a matter of the *collection* of drives feeling pleasure when such commanding is successful. One is "unfree" presumably when there is a feeling of frustration when the commanding drives are not obeyed. One exercises "free will," then, when he or she feels pleasure at a successful command, and one is "unfree" when frustrated.

But this seems a very peculiar sense of free will. Indeed, so peculiar that one is likely to think it is not free will in the slightest bit. After all, Nietzsche had argued against free will on several fronts, and so we should think that he used the term "free will" in some kind of rhetorical way. It is not hard to sympathize with this reaction. But there is something else Nietzsche said in BGE in this connection. At first, it looks as though there is no free will, or, as Nietzsche put it, the correct position is that of "un-freedom of the will.". But, interestingly, he believed that this notion is a "myth" as well. Having eliminated free will, the philosopher should "carry out his 'enlightenment' a step further and to rid himself of this reversal of this misconceived concept of 'free will': I mean the 'un-free will.'" (BGE 21) Philosophers debate about free or unfree will, but "in real life, it is only a matter of *strong* and *weak* wills." (BGE 21) There is a "philosophical ... invention" of free will (GM II: 7), which should be replaced with free and unfree, understood in terms of strong and weak.

Why would we be at all tempted to think a "strong" will is a "free will?" It is plausible to think that those who are "weak" conceive themselves as subjects to all sorts burdens, pressures, and resistances that they are unable to overcome. They are not making changes in the world or in themselves, but other forces are changing *them*. Depression debilitates them; various forces cause them to become impotent in the face of conflicting challenges. They feel themselves at the mercy of things over which they have no power. In *that* sense, they feel themselves "unfree." A strong will—that is to say, one that "commands" in Nietzsche's sense of overcoming resistances—is "free" because those resistances are overcome, and one doesn't feel a victim of external forces.

The suggestion, then, is that we get rid of the previous philosophical interpretations of "free" and "unfree," and instead conceive free will as strong will and unfree as possessing a weak will. Suppose we grant this (and I am not saying it is without its problems). How does that help with the problem of "self-creation" that we reintroduced earlier? One way to think about "self-creation"—and again, I want to stress that this is highly controversial—is not that there is some self who "does" some creating in the sense that sets up the problem in the first place. Recall that there was some single thing about drives, which selects or controls them. Instead, the issue is whether a "self" is created. It is not the self that doing the creating: it is the rather that conditions are such that, fortuitously, a self comes into being. But what does that mean? I have noted repeatedly that, in one sense, the "self" is nothing but a collection of drives. There are two further things I have noted. The first is another apparent paradox, that of "becoming who one is," a notion that starts in *Untimely Meditations*, and is the theme stated in the subtitle of *Ecce Homo*, which is "How one becomes what one is." The second is that there is a Nietzschean refrain of unity. A "single" taste is important in giving style to one's character, whereas when Zarathustra surveys humanity, he says: "I walk among human beings as among the fragments and limbs of human beings" (Z Part I, "On redemption"). So, a suggestion is this: when a *self* is created, there is unity placed upon drives. Here a "self" is understood as unity of drives that is achieved by one dominant drive commanding the others. Right now, most human beings are not like that.

In BGE 200, Nietzsche wrote that

> a human being will have the lineage of multiple lineages in his body, which means conflicting (and often not merely conflicting) drives and value standards that fight with each

other and rarely leave each other alone … [such a human] will typically be a weaker person.

A similar thought is expressed at BGE 208, where conflicting inherited values mean that "both body and soul lack a centre of balance, a centre of gravity." So, the creation of a self would be a matter of a bundle of drives gaining a "center of gravity." This gives a unity to the bundle of drives, but we need to be careful about what "unity" means. Nietzsche noted that human being might seek a "unity" by achieving peace and lack of disturbance. They avoid things, as well as their own drives, achieving a unity of sorts by avoiding their natures. That is not what Nietzsche sought, pointing, instead, to those whose drives are "in conflict and war" and who inherit a "proficiency and finesse in waging war with himself (which is to say: the ability to control and outwit himself)," and are able to cultivate that along his "most powerful and irreconcilable drives." These constitute truly great individuals for Nietzsche because the "ability to control and outwit" is a drive that continues to express *its* power over other powers that are themselves powerful. The unity of a self then is a unity of a single drive continuing to resist, reshape, and overcome other powerful drives. The self is not some endpoint but, instead, the continual activity of the "master" drive.

Nietzsche implied that weak humans lack "freedom of the will" in his sense of the term. People with conflicting drives and no master drive have a will which is "most profoundly sick and degenerate," and "no longer have any sense of independence in decision-making or bold feelings of pleasure in willing,–they doubt whether there is 'freedom of the will', even in their dreams" (BGE 208). Nietzsche's "higher human beings become who they are" because they have, as a matter of fortunate inheritance, a domineering drive that does not deny their drives but seeks to control them, and continually trying to dominate them by putting them into the service of a single goal. As Nietzsche put it in *Twilight of the Idols* in the section entitled "My idea of freedom,"

A free human being is a *warrior*–[Freedom] is measured

by the resistance that needs to be overcome, by the effort that it costs to stay on *top*. Look for the highest type of free human being where the highest resistance is constantly being overcome. [They are like tyrants] if you understand 'tyrant' to mean the merciless and terrible instincts that provoke the maximal amount of authority and discipline against themselves.

None of this presupposes some self behind the drives that is "in control." It is a matter of pure luck that one "inherits," as Nietzsche phrased it, a domineering drive that puts other drives into its service.

Claims about the will to power

We have already mentioned the will to power, and BGE is the published work where doctrine is at its most prominent. In Chapter 2, I discussed Nietzsche's seemingly puzzling claim that drives "aim" at and "value" things and, in the previous chapter, I talked about his claim that every "drive is a kind of lust for domination." I glossed that, seemingly absurd, idea as a view about causal powers: drives are tendencies that maximize effects and so "compete" with other causal powers, redirecting them to their own ends. In BGE 259, Nietzsche repeated his claim that "life" is will to power and, further, that we should grasp psychology "as morphology" and as "the doctrine of the development of the will to power" (BGE 23). We have discussed the former claim, but the latter one again looks very puzzling. Morphology is the study of words and their relations in a given language. How does that relate to psychology and to the will to power? I think what Nietzsche meant is that our values, beliefs, and claims about the world are symptoms or signs of the drives which compose us, each one expressing will to power. As a philologist, Nietzsche saw part of his task as interpreting, which drives some outward belief or claim really expresses. Thus, later in BGE (187), he asked what the particular moral claims tell us about the person who makes them—what an attachment to a morality reveals about the drives of a person. "Morality," he wrote, "is just a sign language of the affects."

There is another claim about the will to power in the BGE, which needs to be noted. In BGE 36, Nietzsche suggested that since we can understand what we do in terms of drives and will to power, then we might perhaps extend this notion of efficacy to the entire world. If "we could trace all organic functions back to the will to power…. then we have earned the right to designate *all* efficacious force as: *will to power*. The world … would just be this 'will to power' and nothing else." This seems to allude to the project that Nietzsche was starting in his unpublished work, that of trying to produce a complete metaphysical picture of the world as nothing but relations of "power quanta." He certainly pursued such a project but, perhaps wisely, abandoned it. His sister, as I have mentioned, turned his notes into a book entitled *The Will to Power*. But it is not something that really impacts on his published work.

6. The Invention of the Sick Animal: *On the Genealogy of Morality*

Nietzsche called *On the Genealogy of Morality* (GM) a "A Polemic. By way of clarification and supplement to my last book Beyond Good and Evil."

I already indicated that GM is a supplement to BGE in the previous chapter. There is a certain kind of morality, a morality of good and evil, which Nietzsche sought to explain (and evaluate), and GM offers an account of the creation of that morality. The account in GM is brilliant, complicated, and immensely subtle, and, as with his other works, it is only possible to give the merest of sketches. It is a "sickness" or a "madness," which potentially leads to a lack of meaning for human existence. The stridency of the language Nietzsche adopted in this work reflects his polemical purposes. He wanted to change our attitude to our morality, and see it as something potentially harmful.

The work comprises a preface and three treatises. The first treatise, "'Good and Evil,' 'Good and Bad,'" describes what is central to the genesis of the values distinctive of modern Western morality. The second, "'Guilt,' 'Bad conscience' and related matters," explains how guilt and bad conscience arise. The third, "What do ascetic ideals mean?" is difficult to explain in a single phrase, so we shall return to that a little later. All three treatises are interconnected as well, thus making pithy summaries rather difficult. Let us begin with the preface.

Questions of morality

Nietzsche mentioned two key questions (GM preface 3). Under what conditions did man invent those value judgments—good and evil? And what value do they themselves have? The second question relates to Nietzsche's overall project of the "re-valuation of values." Our moral values, he thought, are potentially harmful and should themselves be revalued. I will return to this idea at the end of this chapter.

The first question is the primary subject of *GM*, at least in my view, and its task is to explain our morality not as some timeless thing, but as something that the humans have invented. Recall, also from the previous chapter, Nietzsche's belief that there are many *different* moralities and what the GM is primarily, though not exclusively, concerned about is one particular morality, which he variously calls "modern," "slave," "herd," or "Christian," He aimed to explain how that morality emerged and had become dominant. Nietzsche recognized that others had tried to explain morality, but their approaches had been wrongheaded, for a number of reasons, not the least of which is that other philosophers hadn't been sufficiently attuned to historical fact. They tried to explain morality as it was in their time, mistakenly thinking that was how morality had always been. But Nietzsche turned his eye to the ancient world to see a morality rather different from the modern one, trying to show how our morality is a relatively new one that formed in reaction to that ancient one. Now, this fact is important in connection with the task of revaluing values. Unless we become convinced that, at the very least, an alternative morality is possible, let alone that human beings have actually lived by a different morality, then we might find it difficult to conceive of an alternative to our present morality. Modern morality "stubbornly and ruthlessly declares 'I am morality itself and nothing else is moral!'" (BGE 202). I shall return to this, but I want to jump first to the second treatise of GM, which is an attempt to explain something that predates all this and which is fundamental to humanity, namely the notion of a "bad conscience."

The "true problem of man"

All morality is about evaluation, about things, at the greatest level of abstraction, being good, bad, better, worse, right or wrong. It involves standards one can meet, fail to meet, or to which one can aspire. Sometimes, when we fail to do what we should, we suffer from *guilt*, a horrible feeling of moral failure. Nietzsche had a complicated and yet brilliant account of how guilt appears in the human being.

The second treatise opens with a seemingly odd question about how it is possible to "breed an animal which is permitted to make promises." He called this "the true problem of man," and I will explain why that is so. Now, to make a promise involves being able to regulate one's behavior. If I say, "I promise to meet you Tuesday," then I must be able to guide my behavior in accordance with that promise. Nietzsche mentioned that memory is required, which it obviously is, and here he alluded to training by pain. Suppose I am training a dog not to urinate on the carpet. One way to do this is to get the dog to associate pain with the act of urination in that area: every time he urinates, one pulls the scruff of his neck, until he "catches on." His behavior then becomes modified (he remembers the pain) and doesn't urinate on the carpet anymore. There is, however, a key difference between humans and dogs. We can regulate what we do by consciousness *of* something's *being a rule* or its being a *requirement*, whereas the dog does not stop urinating on the carpet because it is conscious of a rule—he has to be *trained* to adopt a certain behavior. Our consciousness of a rule comes with a consciousness of having *failed* to follow a rule, sometimes causing guilt. We are conscious of things being the right thing to do or the wrong thing to do: the dog is not. It learns to behave in ways we think of as right or wrong, but the dog doesn't think in those terms the way we do. To be an animal with a right to make promises, something more is required—namely, consciousness of things being right or required, or better or worse things to do. It requires the animal not merely to be conscious of its environment, as the dog is, but to be also conscious of *itself* as someone attempting to do what is right or required. It needs to be a *self-conscious* or *self-aware* animal. That is the "true problem of man."

We have to wait until GM II: 16 for Nietzsche's explanation of how a self-conscious animal is possible. This is in his account of "bad conscience," that is, painful awareness of one's self-being somehow morally deficient or corrupt. It is a terrible sense of one's self being deeply wrong. Obviously, this is a form of self-awareness, albeit a horrible and painful one. In an outline, Nietzsche explained how such a "gloomy thing" (GM II: 4) comes into being in the following way: prior to bad conscience, humans roamed the environment, governed by instinct. However, Nietzsche supposed, one group enslaved another, imprisoning them in a "state"—not a state in the political sense, but one in which one group of warriors took control of another segment of population. In doing so, the instincts of the enslaved population were curbed. They could no longer express their instincts in the way that they had previously been able to do. Nevertheless, the instincts remained and had to be "discharged;"

Nietzsche claimed that those instincts became part of the enslaved creatures. The central instinct here is the instinct of *cruelty*, of the delight of inflicting pain on others. This instinct, turned on its own possessors, is the origin of bad conscience, and with it comes our basic capacity for self-awareness. Let me explain this extraordinary thought a little further.

Nietzsche highlighted, both earlier in the second treatise of the GM, and in other works, the inescapable fact that human beings enjoy cruelty. It is a fact, furthermore, that fits well with Nietzsche's view that drives express the will to power. In being cruel to another creature, one is dominating and controlling that creature. Cruelty is the key drive that cannot be expressed by those imprisoned in the state, and so they turn against their possessors. There are, no doubt, many ways in which cruelty can be self-directed, but for Nietzsche, the key one was psychological. Self-cruelty leads to the "internalization" of man. That cruelty is turned against one's own drives by being conscious of them as things that are to be hated, despised, or as ugly. One's cruelty is directed at one's self and results in becoming aware of one's self—becoming self-aware in a self-hating way.

> As terrible as bad conscience might be—it is something that introduced a whole new kind of pain into the world—it also signals a "momentous" event. It is a "forceful separation from his [man's] animal past," creating something "new and enigmatic," "full of the future," and with it "first grows in man that which he would later call his 'soul'" (GM II: 16). This is because self-consciousness allows one to consider one's self as a potentially *better* human being, a thing in need of change and improvement. It is, as Nietzsche put it "the true womb of ideal and imaginary events." Humanity cannot aspire to "beauty" without a view of itself as "ugly." "For what would be 'beautiful'.... if the ugly had not first said to itself 'I am ugly.'" (GM II: 18)

Because of bad conscience, the human animal becomes at once both "sick" and "interesting." Interesting because he is now self-aware and able to think in terms of ideals, sick because it is an animal that is now burdened with constant, painful dissatisfaction with itself. It is a creature for whom its existence is "a problem." Bad conscience also brings with it guilt, the painful feeling of having failed in some reprehensible way. Just how that emerges, and its relation to bad conscience is a complicated matter that takes up a good deal of the second treatise. All that I shall say here is that it involves a notion of indebtedness, which, as we shall see when we talk about ascetic ideals, Nietzsche thought was misunderstood in a very serious and harmful way. But there is also the hint of something positive in the second treatise, a figure called "the sovereign individual." Now, this figure is described in such hyperbolic language—he is, for example, called the "lord of free will"—that some commentators, not implausibly, took Nietzsche to be satirizing the ideal of a liberal free individual. But it is striking that this "late fruit," as Nietzsche put it, has not a bad conscience, but a conscience nevertheless. The sovereign individual has "consciousness of power over [himself] and fate, [that] has sunk into his lowest depth and has become instinct, the dominant instinct." (GM II:2) That is to say, he has an evaluative form of self-awareness, but one which is proud rather than wracked with self-hatred. It is not implausible to see this person as the "free" individual we alluded to in the previous chapter, one with a dominant drive, and aware of themselves as such, and without any bad conscience.

Bad conscience yields a capacity to evaluate one's self, and, importantly, it is a negative, painful evaluation. It is virulent among those who have been imprisoned in a "state" by the powerful. Turning now to the first treatise of the GM, Nietzsche worked with a contrast between powerful types—the "masters"—and the oppressed and the weak, that is, the "slaves." The reader will recall that in the previous chapter, I discussed Nietzsche's view of two generic forms of morality, "master" morality and "slave" morality briefly. The "masters" are those who are marked by a confidence, who express their drives in a straightforward manner, in acquisition, conquest, and a great deal more besides. These nobles are taken to be what constitutes "good:" they are highborn, wealthy, and powerful. In contrast, the "slaves" are weak, sick, and, crucially, impotent. They cannot acquire what they need or want and are simply the subjects of the masters. What Nietzsche described here, in an admittedly highly abstract form, were the socio-economic conditions of the ancient world of the West, and the value system it embodied. He tried to explain why that value system became replaced with the one which we now inhabit.

He said that there was a "slave revolt"—not an actual one, but an "imaginary" and "conceptual" one. Impotent and poor slaves cannot

e powerful or rich, but they can think of their poor, impotent
on in new terms. Rather than regarding their impotence as a
negative thing, a lack in comparison to the strength of the masters,
they can think of it as an admirable "peacefulness" or "gentleness."
Timidity and the desperate need for the comfort of others become
instead "meekness" and "kindness." What is previously "bad"
becomes viewed as good. Conversely, the sexual abandon which
the masters can enjoy becomes characterized as animal "lust," their
appetite as "gluttony," and their wealth as "avarice." The goods, and
the masters' capacity to acquire them, now become viewed as
morally bad or "evil."

This slave revolt, as Nietzsche called it, is an "imaginary revenge."
Recall that bad conscience means that human beings are in a
standing state of psychological distress. In Nietzsche's account of
the slave revolt, he added a further, painful, psychological
postulate—that of *ressentiment* (Nietzsche used the French word to
distinguish this state from mere resentment). This is the powerful
pain of frustration or impotence felt by the slaves, a pain brought
about in reaction to things that block their drives, and their
incapacity to gain what the masters possess. Since the slaves cannot
acquire what they want, they suffer *ressentiment*; to be rid of it,
they unconsciously invent this new order of values. They come to
conceive the world in this new way and, in doing so, they reduce the
pain of bad conscience and *ressentiment* because it provides a way
of thinking of themselves as *morally* superior to the nobles.

Further interpretations

The first treatise provokes a number of reactions, including claims
that the account is too abstract or impressionistic. Nietzsche
offered some etymological evidence in support, some allusions to
different cultures but not what one might call detailed historical
evidence. Instead, he accounted for a detectable shift in morality

in terms of general psychological kinds explaining that shift. It is a psychological conjecture about this shift in valuation. In any case, the first treatise is incomplete; Nietzsche elaborated on the GM with the discussion about the figure of the "priest" in the third treatise, and it is to that which we now turn.

As BGE 260 makes clear, the epithets "master" and "slave" characterize many different things and "moralities." One thing they characterize is the general tendency of any person's character. A masterly type is confident and resolute, whereas slave types are uncertain, full of self-doubt, and dependent upon others. The "priest" is another character type, mentioned in the first treatise, but whose crucial role only comes to the fore in the third. The priest type is one who is centrally "hostile to life" (GM III: 11), a hostility that shows itself in condemnation of existence; his practices express withdrawal from the world and, indeed, seem harmful to themselves (Nietzsche mentioned self-flagellation in this connection). The general disposition of the priests is to be repelled by the world in which we live. The priestly type, Nietzsche noted, seemed to embody a paradox, which he expressed as the idea of "life against life" (GM II: 13). How could something be against its own existence, and, indeed, existence itself? But this paradox is merely apparent. The priestly type's hostility to life, his condemnation of existence, expresses something essential to life, namely will to power. The priest expresses his own desire for control and appropriation by giving an overall interpretation of meaning of existence, one which teaches not only the condemnation of this worldly existence, but also the promise of a different form of existence altogether, another world in which the suffering and pain of this one will be left behind. The priest's hostility to life relates to his power because he can offer an interpretation of the constant suffering felt by humanity. He gains control both of himself and others by offering an entire interpretation of human nature and persuades the rest of humanity of it; this interpretation fits rather neatly with the values of the slave revolt.

How? Recall that the *ressentiment* of the slaves led them to invert the values of "master morality." The riches, power, pleasure, and indifference to the general run of humanity of the master types began to be conceptualized as avarice, greed, self-centeredness, gluttony, and lust. The timidity and weakness of the slaves turned into meekness, gentleness, and kindness. This inversion offers imaginary compensation for what is, in fact, the lowly and dispossessed position of the lumpen lot of humanity. Nevertheless, the suffering remains, and the slave's imaginary revolt only goes so far. What the priestly type can do is add to the rebellion an overall interpretation of human existence that justifies the values of the revolt and gives sense to the slaves' suffering. Their negative evaluation of the masters' good fortune fits well with the sense that this world is a temporary place and that there is a greater, spiritual reward waiting in another realm. The truly virtuous deny themselves what is otherwise appealing in this world–power, fortune, satisfaction of our sensual desires–because they "understand" that such things are illusory–mere temptations that beguile the morally weak. The slave's values, born of *ressentiment* directed at the fortunate, are ripe for an interpretation in line with the priest's hostility to life.

But what of the slaves' suffering? Axiomatic to Nietzsche's philosophy is the thesis that human beings cannot bear meaningless suffering, and, by the same token, they can bear any amount of suffering as long as it has a meaning. The priest offers such a meaning by exploiting the ordinary feelings of guilt and the *ressentiment* of the slaves, and by explaining their suffering in terms of sin and corruption. Human nature is inherently corrupt–we have fallen from grace–and we stand guilty before God. But, Nietzsche contended, while this overall interpretation gives meaning to suffering, it does so at the expense of *increasing* suffering. The ordinary misfortunes of the human animal, such as loss, pain, injury, or sickness, are overlaid with guilt and a sense of responsibility, together with a nondischargeable debt to God. The ascetic priest, who presents himself as offering a cure for the sick, actually makes that person sicker.

The ascetic ideal

What has this all to do with modern western morality? The third treatise concerns the "acetic ideal" and what the ideal means for various groups, including artists and philosophers. For reasons of space, I shall not look at what Nietzsche said about artists or philosophers, turning instead to what seems a very surprising claim, namely Nietzsche's view that the ideals of *science* are, in fact, "the last expression" of the ascetic ideal. But to address the question about how all this connects to modern western morality, we need to get some precise grasp of what is meant by the "ascetic ideal."

In GM III: 8, Nietzsche wrote that the ascetic ideal is marked by "three great pomp words:" chastity, poverty, humility. An *ideal* is a goal to which to aspire, and which most of us fail to live up to. Our conception of a saintly figure is someone who lives a life of chastity, poverty, and humility. He is a figure to which to aspire—an ideal—and against whom we can measure our own shortcomings, regulating and improving ourselves. Such an ideal is "life-denying" or "hostile to life." It is against the will to power in the sense that it sets an ideal that is against its straightforward expression: instead, it is an invention of the priest's will to power, his will to provide a dominant interpretation. It "devalues" the dominating and appropriating character of drives. Humble people do not dominate, they do not seek to acquire things or satisfy bodily desire. The saint rejects all those objects of human endeavor, material wellbeing, bodily gratification, and self-interest. The normal human being struggles against these temptations in the light of the ideal set by the saint.

Most humans think this is the morality of the religious. It is a "Christian" morality, with the ideal of the saint, but western morality is now secular. In what way is our morality related to the ascetic ideal? One way to think about this is to see all our values as expressions of the valorization of poverty, chastity and humility, but without being so literal or explicitly religious. Our positive attitudes to selflessness and peacefulness, along with our dislike of arrogance, are secularized forms of humility. Our admiration for frugality, dislike of materialism and of ostentatiousness, represent a form of poverty. Our dislike of promiscuity, and, indeed, the whole complexity of attitudes to sex, is a form of chastity. Morality is about self-denial.

I will return to how and why this might be thought to be problematic. All that I have done so far is give a very brief sketch of Nietzsche's thoughts on how our morality emerges. I mentioned above his belief that science is the last expression of the ascetic ideal. That, on the face of it, seems a bizarre claim. Nietzsche approached it by considering someone who says that science is opposed to such an ideal, partly because science undermines the Christian conception of the universe that underwrites it. What is central to science (and, remember, that the German term—Wissenschaft—means any disciplined knowledge seeking) is the unconditional value it places on truth. Truth is to be obtained at any price, be it helpful or terrible. Ideal scientists are those who sacrifice all in the pursuit of knowledge—"hard, strict, abstinent" types whom Nietzsche described as "heroic" and "pale atheists, anti-Christians." But you will recall that Nietzsche opened *Beyond Good and Evil* by asking just *why* we value truth unconditionally. Or, to put it his way, why there is an unconditional will to truth. He posited that this will is an expression of the ascetic ideal, albeit a "noble" one. This claim has puzzled commentators, but in the GM Nietzsche referred to *The Gay Science* 334, a section entitled "In what way we too are pious." There Nietzsche connected the will to truth with the will not to deceive, and, in particular, the will not to deceive one's self. He suggested that the unconditional will to truth could not be accounted for in terms of usefulness since many truths lack utility, and, more importantly, many truths are dangerous or harmful. Instead, this will stemmed from the "moral ground" that "I will not deceive—even myself." This is connected to the existence of God and, with the Death of God, the question of whether we ought to value truth unconditionally emerges. Even so, this connection is obscure. Nietzsche alluded to the idea that science posits another world, one akin to the Christian heaven, and that truth had been identified with the divine in both the Platonic and Christian traditions. But this doesn't seem yet to connect to the moral claim that "I will not deceive—even myself." Here is a suggestion about the will not to deceive one's self, God, and the will to truth as the expression of the ascetic ideal, though I am not confident that there is enough evidence to support it in the text. God is omniscient, the knower of everything, including, crucially, the knower of the heart of every man and woman. Not deceiving one's self is very important—since God knows your heart, he also knows also your attempts to deny your culpability and evil thoughts. This means we must know our own heart, irrespective of how ugly or awful it might be because we cannot deceive God. Our will to truth becomes unconditional since truth can never, in the end, be escaped.

More about the Death of God

You will notice that I have touched on the Death of God. I have also just referred to a passage that comes from book 5 of *The Gay Science*, and, as I mentioned, this book was coeval with *Beyond Good and Evil* and *On the Genealogy of Morality*. That book opens with a statement of the Death of God, but a statement that seems optimistic. The Death of God brings with it the possibility of truly "free spirits" and an "open sea" of possibility. But there is a different tone in the closing section of the GM. The ascetic ideal, though contributing to the sickness of humanity, has, nevertheless, given man an *ideal*. It has provided an overarching interpretation or significance to human existence, and in particular, its inescapable suffering. Without it we "suffered from an enormous void." Human existence is suffering in many different ways—not only sheer animal suffering, but also suffering from the absence of meaning and from the answer given by the ascetic ideal. Nevertheless, any meaning is better than none, and suffering is bearable when it has a meaning. But in the unconditional pursuit of the truth–itself an expression of the ascetic ideal–those of intellectual conscience can no longer believe in the God who underwrites this meaning, thus destroying the conditions of the "only meaning man has so far had." We understand the ascetic ideal and find that beneath it is "hatred of the human, still more of the animal, still more of the material, ... abhorrence of the senses, of reason itself, ... fear of happiness and beauty, ... looking away from all appearance, change, death, wish, longing itself." For the few, then, there is a very real threat of suicidal nihilism. Humans need an ideal, something to guide the will; otherwise life is impossible. As Nietzsche put it pithily in the final words of the GM, "man would rather will *nothingness* than not will."

Zarathustra, Nietzsche claimed, represents the counter-ideal, he who is "the Anti-Christ, the anti-nihilist; this conqueror of God and of nothingness." (GM II: 24) We talked a little about what the higher type of human being might be like, and how such a person constitutes a new ideal in the chapter on *Thus Spoke Zarathustra*. The GM itself only hints at what this ideal might be (and, it has to be said, Nietzsche was sketchy elsewhere). What the GM does not provide is a side-by-side comparison of slave morality with Nietzsche's counter-ideal. Nietzsche was completely clear in *Ecce Homo*–though some commentators remain stubbornly deaf to his declaration that the GM itself is *not* his revaluation of values but instead constitutes "three decisive *preliminary* studies by a psychologist for a revaluation of all values" (my emphasis). Similarly, he wrote in *The Gay Science* that "the history of origins [of moral judgments] ... is something quite different from a critique" and a "morality of could even have grown out of an error, and realization of this fact would not as much as touch the problem of its value." (GS 345) These "preliminary studies" help to show how the moral culture we inhabit can be seen as a natural product of human psychology and not, therefore, a timeless, fixed thing that constitutes the only possible morality. Once we recognize that, we can consider the possibility of an alternative ideal.

7. Coming to an End: *Twilight of the Idols, The Antichrist, Ecce Homo*, and Wagner Revisited

The year 1888 was extraordinary for Nietzsche. His philosophy was becoming appreciated. At the end of 1887, he was contacted by a Scandinavian professor, Georg Brandes, who was impressed by his work and began lecturing on Nietzsche's philosophy in Copenhagen—lectures that would lead to Nietzsche's eventual acclaim. Nietzsche discovered the northern Italian city of Turin, falling in love with the town (and its ice cream). His physical health improved a little. He had been laboring on what he thought would be his *magnum opus*, which was sometimes entitled *The Revaluation of Values*, and at other times *The Will to Power* (or a combination of the two). Not to be confused with the pseudo-work assembled from his notes by his sister, Nietzsche declared that he abandoned the project in February, though he tinkered with it until August. His preoccupation with Wagner gave birth to *The Case of Wagner* and *Nietzsche contra Wagner*, the latter a compendium of Nietzsche's previous thoughts on the composer. He also wrote three other works: *Twilight of the Idols, or How to Philosophize with a Hammer* (TI), *The Anti-Christ* (A), and *Ecce Homo: How One Becomes What One Is* (EH). The last of these Nietzsche was still working on right up until his fateful breakdown in January 1889, and it was published posthumously in 1908 (TI was published in 1889, A in 1895).

His breakdown naturally raises the question of his mental health in 1888. On the one hand, as I mentioned, he was a little better physically, which seemed to contribute to a sense of giddy exhilaration and megalomaniacal tendencies. But there were signs of his impending collapse. He wrote to Brandes in December, claiming that *The Anti-Christ* was a work of such significance that it would require printing a million copies in every language. In the same month, he stated that he expected a visit from the King and Queen of Italy. These and other signs of mental instability inevitably affect how we understand the writings of his final year. Certainly, *Twilight of the Idols* seems to bear no trace of his breakdown, and his visitors during the period of its composition saw nothing worrisome in his behavior. Some of what Nietzsche wrote in *The Anti-Christ* and in *Ecce Homo* carries with it a question mark. *The Case of Wagner* has its peculiarities, but it doesn't seem out of tune with Nietzsche's general attitude to the composer who, he thought, was symptomatic of the decline of culture. His critique makes use of the concept of "decadence," one that is important in the writings of that year, and to which we shall return. We turn first to *Twilight of the Idols*.

"A declaration of war"

The title of *Twilight of the Idols* is, as many have observed, a play on Wagner's *Twilight of the Gods*. Its subtitle, *How to Philosophize with a Hammer*, can mislead, making one think of Nietzsche as engaged in wanton destruction, an orgy of smashing. But it is too a musical reference, a matter of "tapping" idols to see if they are hollow or cracked, the hammer being akin to a tuning fork. The philosopher (Nietzsche) is examining those idols with "an evil ear" (TI preface). It is, he wrote, "a declaration of war" and part of his project of the "revaluation of values" (TI preface). The preface is dated September 30, 1888, which he declared as the day he finished the first book of the *Revaluation of Values*—*The Anti-Christ*.

This work touches on many subjects, though it is certainly more compact and focused than some other of his works. It is perhaps the best distillation of his mature philosophy, and yet recalls themes from *The Birth of Tragedy*. It was written, reportedly, at a tremendous pace but without seeming to suffer from that fact. Its opening section, "Arrows and Epigrams," contains pithy aphorisms (Nietzsche at his most quotable), and is followed by "The Problem of Socrates." The reader will recall that in *The Birth of Tragedy*, Nietzsche pointed the finger at "Socratism" as a philosophy that killed the redemptive character of Greek Tragedy, and there are echoes of this claim in this chapter. Socrates, Nietzsche claimed, was decadent. Decadence was a concept of great currency in the late 19th century, informing a whole school of art. At a first approximation, it signaled a kind of moral decline and a collapse into hedonism. Nietzsche would certainly not see mere voluptuousness as a welcome thing, but moral decline for him was obviously a rather more complicated matter. The kind of decline Nietzsche had in mind was the threat of nihilism, as humanity suffered increasingly from a lack of meaning. Humans are sets of drives, and without some ideal, there is psychic and cultural anarchy. Socrates represented a rejection of dominant instinct, both personally and culturally, and the honoring of dialect—of the method of question and answer—behind which is little but rabble-rousing *ressentiment*. Cold reason doesn't cure the human condition, Nietzsche posited, but instead puts human beings at war with their own instincts. It is a "fight" against the instincts.

Nietzsche identified these problems in some artists and thinkers whom he named and criticized in "Skirmishes of an Untimely Man" and saw the problem endemic in certain conceptions of the German character ("What the Germans Lack"). Under the title of "Morality as Anti-Nature," Nietzsche returned to this fight against the instincts. The reader will recall that bad conscience is the sickness caused by instincts turned against themselves. One "cure" is the Christian interpretation of our nature, which includes the idea that many of our instincts are base, merely animal and not part of our "real" nature. Therefore, our instincts are to be denied, destroyed, and extirpated. This is a key sense in which morality is "anti-nature." But in this section, Nietzsche offered an alternative, positive proposal, which is to harness our natures rather than to deny them. This is the notion of the "spiritualization" or "sublimation" of the instincts (a notion which was to become central to Freud's philosophy). To sublimate a drive is not to reject or extirpate it, but instead redirect it to another object, and in doing so shape that very drive. Nietzsche gave two examples, the sublimation of sensuality into love, and hostility into valuing the existence of enemies. In both cases, the basic expression and its aim in its object alters. Mere sex drive is turned into a deeper appreciation of the other, and hostility is turned into an appreciation of enemies as an object of resistance over which the will to power can exercise itself. This is in line with Nietzsche's view that we constantly reinterpret our drive-based tendencies and offer them new meanings. Our sex drive is not destroyed but given a new, healthier expression. Though Nietzsche didn't explicitly say it, such sublimation is part of what it means to create new values. As mentioned before, Nietzsche saw the world as valueless and values were created by the drives being directed towards objects. Sublimation is a matter of the very same drive producing a more nuanced and subtle conception of its objects, creating richer and more subtle values.

Nietzsche also offered his "first example" of the revaluation of values (TI, Four Great Errors, 2). He claimed that all moralities and religions prior to him saw happiness as coming from following certain prescriptions. Happiness was conceived as a reward for good behavior. Nietzsche's first example of the revaluation of values is that the truth is precisely the opposite. The capacity for generosity, for example, requires someone who exhibits the kind of self-determination and order of the drives which Nietzsche found so admirable. He or she can deal well with others, rather than slavishly following the dictates of morality in hopes of reward. Nietzsche's conception of happiness was not that of the "last men," seeking contentment and a balance of pleasure over pain, but instead, those who, through a coincidence of drives and circumstance, have a single overarching goal to which all their drives are harnessed.

This can all sound rather homely, as it were. Harness one's drives in a healthy way and tend to your own wellbeing first to ensure you can help others. But it leaves open the question of how that might be achieved. One thing that is clear in Nietzsche's writing, and rather unpalatable to modern ears, is his belief that only aristocratic, rather than democratic, orders are conducive to the flourishing of such higher types. For him, democracy was the political outgrowth of the morality of *ressentiment*, the aim of which was to devalue the higher types, and create a modest working class, trained not to aspire to anything but to be self-sufficient in their work, allowing the great to flourish. A further problem lurks in Nietzsche's account. In inveighing against slave morality and its focus of selflessness, didn't he give license to individuals whose selfishness is horrific? It is unclear what Nietzsche could say in response to this; certainly, he didn't want his immoralism to be a free-for-all. In *Daybreak* 103, for example, he wrote that it "goes without saying that I do not deny–unless I am a fool–that many actions called immoral ought to be avoided and resisted, or that many called moral oughts to be done and encouraged." He added that they should be done for "other reasons than hitherto." But it remains unclear just why that is so or what constraints there are on what is to be done or not done. I suspect Nietzsche thought that since each higher type set their own goals and standards, then it would be impossible to codify some set of restrictions that are to be placed on them. Nietzsche praised Goethe as an incomparable individual who "created himself" (TI, Skirmishes of an Untimely Man, 49). But there is a question mark about whether some darker individuals might go beyond good and evil in a far less attractive way.

Declining mental state

The subtitle of *The Anti-Christ* was going to be *The Revaluation of Values* until a last-minute switch to A *Curse of Christianity*, a change that perhaps reflects Nietzsche's rapidly declining mental state. The title itself is, as so many of Nietzsche's titles, potentially misleading. It could equally be translated as *The Anti-Christian*, and this would be perhaps the better translation, since Nietzsche seemed to hold Jesus Christ in some regard, reserving his sternest invective for St. Paul. Section 2 of the work could be an all-too-brief summary of Nietzsche's revaluation of values. Good is what enhances the feeling of power; bad is that which stems from weakness. Happiness is the activity of power–"the feeling of power growing." That much is familiar, but Nietzsche added, provocatively, that the "new principle" of the "love of humanity" is that the "weak and the failures should" perish, and what is more harmful than any vice is "pity for weakness and failures." This was Nietzsche at his most hyperbolic, perhaps intimating his imminent collapses again.

Jesus Christ himself, according to Nietzsche at any rate, was not a "miracle worker and redeemer," nor one who invented a reality of heaven beyond this world, but someone whose practice and behavior "towards the henchmen, the way he acted in the face of his accusers and every type of slander and derision" (A 35) constituted an example of how to live. His "kingdom of heaven" is a psychological one, and his death is "not a bridge" to another world. Jesus himself was a unique psychological type. However, this "symbolism" became embroiled in the psychology of *ressentiment*. St. Paul represents the opposite of Jesus as "the bringer of glad tidings." It was he who concocted the myth of the resurrection and a life beyond this world in order to gain power and offer an interpretation of human existence to support it. Nietzsche saw St. Paul as a concrete example of the priestly type we met in *On the Genealogy of Morality*. In connection with this, *The Anti-Christ* also contains some of Nietzsche's most unequivocal statements in favor of science as the route to truth. Priests "can only imagine one great danger: and that is science" (A 49). Key here is Nietzsche's view that religion rests on a faulty conception of cause and effect, a theme that comes up in this work, as well as in the *Twilight of the Idols*. Phenomena like bad conscience and guilt are given interpretations of their causal origins, which are false. Guilt is not "the voice of God in man," as he put in *Ecce Homo*.

This brings us to *Ecce Homo*, and the question of Nietzsche's sanity. It is an autobiography of an extraordinary sort. The hyperbole of its section titles is evident. We have "Why I am so Wise," "Why I am So Clever," "Why I Write Such Good Books," and "Why I am a Destiny." These titles could be taken as indications of Nietzsche's deteriorating mental state, on the one hand, or as satire on the very business of autobiography, on the other. Some of the claims he made in EH are pure fiction. He claimed to be descended from Polish nobility through his father's side (his relationship with his mother and his sister was very poor at the time he wrote the work). "I am," he wrote, "a pure-blooded Polish nobleman without a drop of bad blood" (EH, Why I am So Wise 3). Again, such a preposterous claim can be read two ways: either, again, as a sign of his mental decline, or a rhetorical device to distance himself from contemporary Germany, which he saw as culturally decadent and jingoistic. The summaries of his works are not up to what one might expect from him, including the fact that he devoted most ink to discussing *Thus Spoke Zarathustra*. His letters, though, written at about the same time, seem, as I mentioned, to exhibit incipient megalomania. Philosophically, there are familiar themes from his previous works but presented in ways that require the reader to have a prior grasp of his work.

It is, I think, difficult to discern the extent to which Nietzsche's illness affected *Ecce Homo*. The title of the work itself—"behold the man"—is a reference to what Roman procurator of Judea Pontius Pilate supposedly declared on seeing Christ in his crown of thorns prior to his crucifixion, and many works of art were produced bearing that title. For Nietzsche, the title played on a contrast between the ideal ascetic type of Christianity and Nietzsche's own alternative, Dionysos. The final line of the work is "Have I been understood?—*Dionysos verses the crucified*" (EH, Why I am a Destiny 9). In telling us why he is a destiny, he elaborated on this contrast by explaining in what his "immoralism" consisted. He negated a human ideal, that of the benevolent and charitable, and the ascetic, Christian morality, which we have considered in various places in this book. He repeated his idea that such a morality encourages the "last men"–the type who values docile contentment and freedom from suffering. Such types "live at the expense of the *truth* as much as they live at the expense of the *future*" (EH, Why I am a Destiny 4). As well as Dionysos, this is another call back to *The Birth of Tragedy*. What is needed is the type who "conceives reality *as it is*," and "everything terrible and questionable" about it (EH, Why I am a Destiny 5). *The Birth of Tragedy* required us to confront the awful character of existence but through the aesthetic lens of tragedy. Here Nietzsche appeared simply to think in terms of someone strong enough to affirm reality while grasping it as it really is.

But what of the book's subtitle? How does one become what one is? We discussed this topic in the chapter on *Beyond Good and Evil*, but *Ecce Homo* adds a little to the basic thesis, explaining how Nietzsche became who he is. He described himself as decadent, particularly in terms of his own physical sickness. But this illness allowed him to be the opposite of decadent, for it furnished him with a will to spiritual health. It allowed for his change of perspective, a shift from the nihilism of his Wagner/Schopenhauer period to his more affirmative philosophy. Nietzsche attempted to describe in general "how one becomes what one is" in Why I am So Clever, 9. Those looking for instructions, however, will be disappointed. Its lead motif is that there must be some organizing drive–works at the unconscious level–and becoming "what you are presupposes you have not the slightest idea of *what* you are." Consciousness needs to be free of misconceptions of one's self, which might interfere with instincts. What is central to this "organizing" idea is selfishness, which is presumably a matter of its co-opting other drives in its direction. So, self-creation, as I suggested a few chapters ago, is more a matter of luck or fate than the expression itself might seem to suggest. Nietzsche's life, as he suggested, had been a series of fortunes and misfortunes, which finally led to the appropriate conditions for the flourishing of its nature. Perhaps what Nietzsche was really expressing was his own "formula for human greatness," as he called it in the next section. Not "to want anything to be different, not forwards, not backwards, not for all eternity. Not just to tolerate necessity, still less to conceal it ... all idealism is hypocrisy towards necessity–but to *love* it." One can only hope that this attitude survived the fate that would befall Nietzsche mere weeks after writing that sentence when his capacity to reason left him.

8. Nietzsche's Legacy

It is rather difficult to write about Nietzsche's legacy. Returning to a point I made in the Preface, his writings are complex and yet have a powerful attraction. That is why his works have been read—and often *mis*read—in different, and utterly contradictory, ways. Indeed, in some cases "read" might be too strong a word: "cherry-picked" is perhaps more fitting. Nietzsche anticipated being misunderstood, which might explain why the closing sections of *Ecce Homo* each begin with the question "Have I been understood?"

So, Nietzsche has a legacy of being misunderstood in all languages into which his writings had been translated, and in practically every country where his books had been published. His ideas were discussed in Japan at the beginning of the 20th century, even though no translations of his works in Japanese were then available. In Uruguay in 1900, essayist José Rodó repudiated the Übermensch in his essay *Ariel*, while in Peru in 1928, philosopher José Mariátegui made a Marxist hero out of Nietzsche. In China, interest in his thoughts began at about the same time as it did in Japan, only to be suppressed when the communists came to power. The playwright George Bernard Shaw authored the play *Man and Superman*, bringing the Übermensch and Don Juan together on the stage in 1902. In France, much later in the 1970s, some remarks of Nietzsche's about truth and interpretation were imaginatively spun into something dubbed the "New Nietzsche," which appeared resolutely set against taking Nietzsche at his repeated word about facts, psychology, and experience. French philosopher Sarah Kofman wrote several books centered on her reading of Nietzsche, intertwined with Freud and feminism. A Holocaust survivor and defender of Nietzsche against the charge of antisemitism, Kofman read his books along the lines of the "New Nietzsche" in a rather intimate way. Curiously, she committed suicide on the 150th anniversary of Nietzsche's death.

In America, the conservative critic Allan Bloom wrote an article entitled "How Nietzsche Conquered America," which, while admitting that Nietzsche is difficult to understand, pins the blame for something he calls "value-relativism"–the crude idea that no values are better than others–lamenting that "un-American ideas took root in America. More recently, psychologist Steven Pinker managed spectacularly to misunderstand the Enlightenment and failed to recognize that Nietzsche comprehended the movement and its implications. Instead, Pinker preferred to think Nietzsche recommended a life without feeling and conscience. Another psychologist, Jordan Peterson, found inspiration in Nietzsche in his campaign against the left, while somehow still extolling the values of Christianity.

One could go on, almost endlessly, about the impact of Nietzsche's works on people with very different values and dispositions, and if that is his legacy, it is, as I mentioned, misunderstood. What Nietzsche deserves is not another attempt to make him a poster boy or *bête noire* for someone else's project by appealing to pithy quotations, but instead the effort, which is now thankfully being made, to understand him on his own terms. Nietzsche knew the dangers that stem from his writings, but he claimed that the fault was not necessarily his. Modern man, he noted, lacks a quality that cows have which is necessary for him to be understood–rumination.

Sources

BT – *The Birth of Tragedy and Other Writings*, ed. Geuss and Spiers, Cambridge, 1999

UT – *Untimely Meditations*, ed. Breazeale, Cambridge, 1997

HAH – *Human, All Too Human*, ed. Hollingdale and Schacht, Cambridge, 1986

D – *Daybreak*, ed. Clark and Leiter, Cambridge, 1997

GS – *The Gay Science*, ed. Williams, Cambridge, 2001

Z – *Thus Spoke Zarathustra*, ed. Pippin and Del Caro, Cambridge, 2006

BGE – *Beyond Good and Evil*, ed. Horstmann and Norman, Cambridge, 2002

GM – *On the Genealogy of Morality*, ed. Clark and Swensen, Hackett, 1998

TI – *Twilight of the Idols*, ed. Ridley and Norman, Cambridge, 2005

A – *The Anti-Christ*, ed. Ridley and Norman, Cambridge, 2005

EH – *Ecce Homo*, ed. Ridley and Norman, Cambridge, 2005

WP – *The Will to Power*, ed. Kaufmann, Vintage, 1968

Suggested Reading

There has been so much written on Nietzsche that it is hard to know where to begin, but two biographical studies can be suggested. Julian Young's biography, *Nietzsche: A Philosophical Biography* (Cambridge, 2010), though enormous, is very readable, and doesn't demand too much from those unfamiliar with philosophy as an academic discipline. Lesley Chamberlin's *Nietzsche in Turin* (Quarter, 1996) is a very engaging account of Nietzsche's last sane year.

When it comes to interpreting Nietzsche's philosophy, so much has been written about this subject, but a lot of it is of dubious quality. The introductory material to each of the works listed in the sources section of this book is, on the whole, pretty good, though some of it might be taxing for the non-specialist. Robert Solomon and Kathleen Higgins *What Nietzsche Really Said* (Schocken, 2000) doesn't live up to its title (few books could), but it is readable and not too misleading. For a look at what first-rate scholarship on Nietzsche looks like, the reader could not do better than Gemes and Richardson (eds.) *The Oxford Handbook of Nietzsche* (Oxford, 2013).

About the Author

Peter Kail is Associate Professor in Philosophy at the University of Oxford and Official Fellow and Tutor in Philosophy. He is the author of *Projection and Realism in Hume's Philosophy* (2007) and co-editor of *Nietzsche on Mind and Nature* (2015). He is a founder member of the International Nietzsche Society and serves on its executive committee.

Afterword

Thank you for reading *Simply Nietzsche*!

If you enjoyed reading it, we would be grateful if you could help others discover and enjoy it too.

Please review it with your favorite book provider such as Amazon, BN, Kobo, iBooks or Goodreads, among others.

Again, thank you for your support and we look forward to offering you more great reads in the future.

CPSIA information can be obtained
at www.ICGtesting.com
Printed in the USA
LVHW040537280120
645023LV00006B/779